Justice, Primitive and Modern

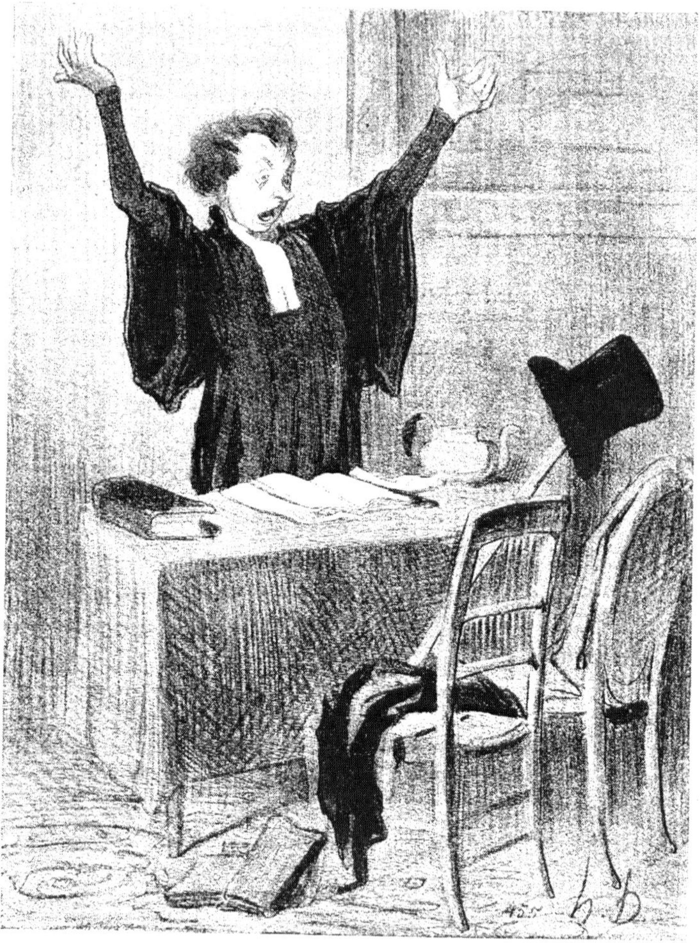

Justice, Primitive and Modern

Dispute Resolution in Anarchist and State Societies

Bob Black

NINE-BANDED BOOKS

Justice, Primitive and Modern
By Bob Black

🄯

Copyleft, 2023
All rites reversed

Published by

Nine-Banded Books
PO Box 1862
Charleston, WV 25327
USA

www.NineBandedBooks.com

Cover design by Kevin I. Slaughter

Contents

Author's Note
~ 7

Introduction
~ 9

1. Forms of Dispute Resolution
~ 15

2. Case Studies
~ 27

3. Multiplex Relationships
~ 37

4. Forms of Dispute Resolution
~ 39

5. The Politics of Informal Justice
~ 41

6. Conclusions for Reformists
~ 61

7. The Inclomplete Anarchist Critique of Criminal Law
~ 65

8. "Restorative Justice"
~ 89

9. "Regenerative Shaming"
~ 127

10. The Anarchist Academics: A Sorry Story
~ 137

Author's Note

A much shorter, much different version of this text, under the title "Justice: Primitive and Modern," was delivered as a speech at a B.A.S.T.A.R.D. Conference in Berkeley, California. Some years later, on August 14, 2015, a closer version was delivered as a speech at the Pontifical and Royal University of Santo Tomas, under the auspices of its Philosophy Department, in Manila, Philippines. Among the others who have spoken at that site (the Thomas Aquinas Research Center) was then U.S. Secretary of State Hillary Rodham Clinton, later a defeated candidate for President. This version is thoroughly revised, greatly expanded and referenced. The material on Restorative Justice is new.

Introduction

IN ALL SOCIETIES, there's some trouble between people. Most societies have processes for resolving disputes. These include negotiation, mediation, arbitration and adjudication.[1] In their pure forms, negotiation and mediation are voluntary. Arbitration and adjudication are involuntary.[2] The ethnographic evidence shows "pretty strongly . . . that adjudicatory decision-making as opposed to mediatory activity is almost exclusively linked to the presence of central government."[3] The voluntary processes are typical of anarchist societies, since anarchist societies are voluntary societies. The involuntary processes are typical of state societies. In all societies there are also self-help remedies.[4] These are often effective as social

---

1 Donald Black with M.P. Baumgartner, "Toward a Theory of the Third Party," in Donald Black, *The Social Structure of Right and Wrong* (San Diego, CA: Academic Press, 1993), 110–115 (originally 1983).

2 Actually, there is voluntary and involuntary arbitration: "When arbitration is in no sense binding, both in the sense that the two parties must go to arbitration on the demand of either and must then abide by the arbitrator's holdings, it tends to merge into judicial judgment." If it is not binding it tends to merge into mediation. Martin Shapiro, *Courts: A Comparative and Political Analysis* (Chicago, IL & London: University of Chicago Press, 1981), 4.

3 Simon Roberts, "The Study of Dispute: Anthropological Perspectives," in *Disputes and Settlements: Law and Human Relations in the West*, ed. John Bossy (Cambridge: Cambridge University Press, 1983), 15.

4 Laura Nader & Harry F. Todd, Jr., "Introduction: The Disputing Process," in *The Disputing Process—Law in Ten Societies*, ed. Laura Nader & Harry F. Todd, Jr. (New York: Columbia University Press, 1978), 9–10. Despite the title of their book, they profess neutrality as to "the question whether these procedures are law or social control or 'merely' custom." Ibid., 8. "The tendency to dissolve the idea of law into the

control, but they only provide justice when might and right happen to coincide. In primitive societies, peace, not justice, is the highest priority.

The voluntary processes deal with a dispute as a problem to be solved. They try to reach an agreement between the parties which restores social harmony, or at least keeps the peace. The involuntary processes implicate law and order, crime and punishment, torts, breaches of contracts, and in general, rights and wrongs. The difference interests me, among other reasons, because I'm an anarchist who lives in a statist society. I'm also a former lawyer. It is hard not to agree with E.B. Tylor, who wrote that "one of the most essential things we can learn from the life of rude tribes is how society can function without the policemen to keep order."[5]

I argue that voluntary processes are more effective in primitive societies, where there may be no peaceable alternatives, than in state societies. But in any society, the justice of private settlement might be more effective than the justice of the courts, since the only certain way of ending a dispute is to convince both parties that an end has been reached.[6] The question is: which outcome is more convincing? There will always be

---

broader notion of social control is pervasive in the sociological and anthropological literature." Philippe Nonet & Philip Selznick, *Law and Society in Transition: Toward Responsive Law* (New York: Harper Colophon Books, 1978), 10 n. 11. Many people, including myself, draw a sharp distinction between law (regarded as statist) and custom (regarded as anarchist). *E.g.*, Donald Black, *The Behavior of Law* (New York: Academic Press, 1976), 2 (defining law as "governmental social control"); Stanley Diamond, "The Rule of Law versus the Order of Custom," in *The Rule of Law*, ed. Robert Paul Wolff (New York: Simon & Schuster, Touchstone Books, 1971), 116–17, reprinted in Stanley Diamond, *In Search of the Primitive: A Critique of Civilization* (New Brunswick, NJ: Transaction Books, 1974), 257–58; ibid., "The Search for the Primitive," 136–37. A prominent rejection of the idea that "a distinguishing mark of law consists in the use of coercion or force" is Lon L. Fuller, *The Morality of Law* (rev. ed.; New Haven, CT & London: Yale University Press, 1969), 108.

5 Edward B. Tylor, *Anthropology: An Introduction to the Study of Man and Civilization* (New York: D. Appleton & Co., 1907), 405.

6 Jenny Formald, "An Early Modern Postscript: The Sandlow Dispute, 1546," in *The Settlement of Disputes in Early Medieval Europe*, ed. Wendy Davies & Paul Fouracre (Cambridge: Cambridge University Press, 1986), 192. As discussed below, state-sponsored, ostensibly voluntary processes are often ineffective, judging by their substantial rates of recidivism.

some grievants who remain unconvinced, and some conflicts which later resume, under any system.

Adjudication always, according to Martin Shapiro, raises an issue of the legitimacy of authority, because the loser may perceive that he has merely been ganged up on by an enemy allied to a power wielder.[7] It doesn't occur to this political scientist that state authority as such raises a question of legitimacy. Political philosophers often justify it, sometimes half-guiltily, by positing a "social contract." Setting aside the absurdities of all versions of this theory, which even many philosophers acknowledge, for my purposes I only want to draw attention to the underlying assumption: that consent confers authority. In a state society, "tacit consent" supposedly legitimates the state—any state: democratic, fascist, state communist, theocratic, whatever.[8]

Of course this tacit "consent" bears no resemblance to what consent means in everyday life, where it refers to actual, conscious, individual, informed agreement to or about specific actions. Try to imagine a claim of tacit consent to get married. And marriage, unlike government, really is a contract! Anarchists like Lysander Spooner and libertarians like Herbert Spencer have debunked tacit consent.[9] So did David Hume, who was no anarchist or libertarian.[10]

"Tacit consent" is wholesale consent, imputed consent:

---

[7] Martin Shapiro, *Courts: A Comparative and Political Analysis* (Chicago, IL: University of Chicago Press, 1986), 3. Adjudication is typically initiated by a grievant, not by the decision-maker. John Chipman Gray, *The Nature and Sources of the Law* (2nd ed.; New York: Macmillan, 1921), 114–115.

[8] Bob Black, "Debunking Democracy," *Defacing the Currency: Selected Writings 1992–2012* (Berkeley, CA: LBC Books, 2012), 32 n. 75.

[9] Lysander Spooner, "No Treason. No. 6. The Constitution of No Authority," in *No Treason: The Constitution of No Authority and A Letter to Thomas Bayard* (Novato, CA: Libertarian Publishers, n.d.), 5: Herbert Spencer, *Social Statics* (New York: Robert Schaltenbach Foundation, 1954), 90; see Bob Black, *Nightmares of Reason* (2009–2015), ch. 17, available online at www.theanarchistlibrary.org.

[10] David Hume, "Of the Original Contract," *Essays: Moral, Political, and Literary*, ed. Eugene F. Miller (rev. ed.; Indianapolis, IN: Liberty Fund, [1987]), 465–487. Agreeing with Hume is Adam Smith, *Lectures on Jurisprudence* (Indianapolis, IN: Liberty Fund, 1982), 321, 402–403.

consent to the state and to whatever it does, including adjudication, which can be one of the less bad things the state does. This tacit consent to anything, of which the loser is completely unaware (because it's only "tacit"), is not something which will mollify the loser of a civil case, much less the loser of a criminal case.

In contrast, in anarchist societies, consent is retail, not wholesale. Everything is voluntary, although voluntary actions are often subject to the informal influence of others. This will be apparent in the case studies which follow. In these societies, one or both parties may in principle reject mediation (this rarely happens), and either party may reject a mediated settlement, but this only occasionally happens. This is consent on specific occasions to specific procedures and settlements. This is real consent. It is reasonable to believe that, in general, these voluntary mediated settlements, where that is the procedure, more often finally settle disputes than adjudication does, where that is the procedure.

Most modern anarchists, like most other moderns, are ignorant of how disputes are resolved in stateless primitive societies. And they rarely talk about how disputes would be resolved in their own modern anarchist society. This is a major reason why anarchists aren't taken seriously. I have a lesson for the anarchists. But I also have a lesson for modern legal reformers. Using examples, I'll discuss disputing in several primitive stateless societies. Then I'll discuss an attempt to reform the American legal system which was supposedly inspired by the disputing process used in one African tribal society. The idea was to insert a version of mediation into the bottom layer of the U.S. legal system at the discretion of judges and prosecutors. It was a failure. I will come to the conclusion that you can't graft an essentially voluntary procedure onto an essentially coercive legal system.

If I'm right, the case for anarchy is strengthened at its weakest point: how to maintain a generally safe and peaceful society without a state. Many anthropologists have remarked upon this achievement.[11] Not many anarchists have. The controversy over anarchist "primitivism" has been almost entirely pointless, because it goes off on such issues as technology, population, and the pros and cons of various cultural consequences of civilization (religion, writing, money, the state, the class system, high culture, etc.). The possibility that certain structural features of primitive anarchy might be viable in— indeed, may be constitutive of—*any* anarchist society, primitive or modern, has received no attention from any anarchist. Primitivists urge anarchists to learn from the primitives[12]—but learn *what*? How to build a sweat lodge?

---

11 *E.g.,* E. Colson, "Social Control and Vengeance in Plateau Tonga Society," *Africa* 23(3) (July 1953), 199–200, reprinted as chapter 3 of Elizabeth Colson, *The Plateau Tonga of Northern Rhodesia: Social and Religious Studies* (Manchester, England: Manchester University Press, 1962); Diamond, "The Rule of Law versus the Order of Custom," 135; R.F. Barton, *Ifugao Law* (Berkeley & Los Angeles, CA: University of California Press, 1969), "Preface" (n.p.) & 3 (originally 1919).

12 *E.g.,* A. Morfus, "Beyond Utopian Visions," in *Uncivilized: The Best of Green Anarchy* (n.p.; Green Anarchy Press, 2012).

1. Forms of Dispute Resolution

WHEN A CONFLICT ARISES between individuals—whether or not it later draws in others—initially, and usually, it may be resolved privately by discussion. Negotiation, a bilateral procedure, is undoubtedly a universal practice[1]: "It is the primary mode of handling major conflicts in many simple societies throughout the world."[2] In the terminology I adopt here,[3] where a conflict is resolved by negotiation, there has been a conflict but not a dispute. There is first a *grievance*: someone feels wronged. If she expresses her grievance to the wrongdoer, she makes a *claim*. If she gets no satisfaction, she has several alternatives. She may take unilateral action, actively or passively. The active way, "self-help," is to coerce or punish the wrongdoer, but, sadly, that is often not feasible.[4] Nonetheless, where real alternatives scarcely exist, as in the inner

---

[1] P.H. Gulliver, "Case Studies of Law in Non-Western Societies: Introduction," in *Law and Culture in Society*, ed. Laura Nader (Berkeley, CA: University of California Press, 1997), 21 (originally 1969).

[2] Donald Black, "The Elementary Forms of Conflict Management," *Social Structure of Right and Wrong*, 83.

[3] Ibid., 14; Frank E.A. Sander, "Varieties of Dispute Processing," in Roman M. Tomasic & Malcolm M. Feeley, eds., *Neighborhood Justice: Assessment of an Emerging Idea* (New York & London: Longman, 1982), 38 n. 4 (originally1976); Richard E. Miller & Austin Sarat, "Grievances, Claims, and Disputes: Assessing the Adversary Culture," *Law & Society Rev.* 15(3, 4) (1980–1981): 525–566.

[4] But it is more common than is generally believed. Donald Black, "Crime as Social Control," in *Towards a General Theory of Social Control*, ed. Donald Black (Orlando, FL: Academic Press, 1984), 2: 1–27, reprinted in *Social Structure of Right and Wrong*, 27–46; Black, "'Wild Justice': Crime as an Anarchist Source of Social Order," 233–267.

city, some people resort to violent unilateral retaliation.[5] The passive way is "lumping it": caving, doing nothing.[6] This is how many grievances, instead of rising to the level of disputes, fall into oblivion. "You can't fight city hall" or various other too-powerful oppressors. Lumping it—avoidance—may also be universal, but it's especially common in the simplest and in the most complex societies: among hunter-gatherers and also in statist class societies with vast power disparities.[7]

As useful as negotiation can be, it doesn't always work. It doesn't always produce agreement. Dyads may deadlock. Whereas in a triad, the decision might be made by majority rule, or through mediation.[8] Or feelings may run so high that the parties refuse to talk to each other, or if they do, the encounter may turn violent.[9] And negotiation isn't always fair, because disputants are never exactly equal. If one party has a more forceful personality or a higher social status or more wealth or more connections, a settlement of the dispute is likely to favor him unduly. Among the rationales for involving a third party—whether a mediator, an arbitrator, or a judge—is to equalize the process by bringing in a participant who is impartial and independent. However, impartiality is the ideal but not always the reality of mediation. [10] The third party may also serve as a face-saving device for acquiescence in a settlement which, if negotiated bilaterally, might appear to be (and might actually be) a surrender to the other side.

---

[5] Elijah Anderson, *Code of the Street: Decency, Violence, and the Moral Life of the Inner City* (New York: W.W. Norton & Co., 1999); Black, "Crime as Social Control."

[6] William L.F. Felsteiner, "Influences of Social Organization on Dispute Processing," in *Neighborhood Justice*, 54.

[7] M.P. Baumgartner, *The Moral Order of a Suburb* (New York & Oxford: Oxford University Press, 1988), 11.

[8] "Mediation—Its Forms and Functions," in *The Principles of Social Order: Selected Essays of Lon L. Fuller*, ed. Kenneth I. Winston (Durham, NC: Duke University Press, 1981), 133; see also *The Sociology of Georg Simmel*, ed. Kurt Wolff (New York: The Free Press, 1950), 118–169.

[9] Simon Roberts, *Order and Dispute: An Introduction to Legal Anthropology* (Oxford, England: Martin Robertson, 1979), 72.

[10] Gulliver, "On Mediators," 16, 46.

If the victim (as she sees herself) voices her grievance to third parties, now there is a *dispute* which implicates, if only in a minor way, the interests of society. A dispute is an "activated complaint."[11] The appeal, whether explicit or implicit, depending on the individual and the society, might mean calling the police, filing a lawsuit, or just complaining to people you know. It might mean going to court—the court of law or the court of public opinion. Mediation (voluntary) and adjudication (compulsory) are distinguishable from negotiation and self-help inasmuch as they necessarily involve a third party who has no personal interest in the outcome of the dispute.[12] Mediation could be considered assisted negotiation.[13]

Some primitive societies—especially the smallest-scale societies, the band societies of hunter-gatherers—have no customary dispute resolution processes. Contrary to some statements,[14] "triadic" dispute processes are not universal. In band societies, not only is there no authority, there is no procedure for resolving disputes or facilitating settlements: no mediator or arbitrator.[15] Thus, among the Bushmen, interpersonal quarrels usually arise suddenly and publicly, in camp. They range from arguments and mockery to fighting, which is usually restrained by others who are present, but which occasionally turns deadly. Anyone may use lethal force to settle a dispute. If the dispute gives rise to ongoing enmity between individuals (and their associates), often one of the disputants moves away to join another band (this often happens anyway); or sometimes the local band separates into two.[16] This is typ-

---

11 W.L.F. Felstiner, Richard Abel, & Austin Sarat, "The Emergence and Transformation of Disputes: Naming, Blaming, Claiming . . . ," *Law & Society Rev.* 15 (1980–1981), 635–37.

12 Felsteiner, "Influences of Social Organization on Dispute Processing," 48.

13 *Social Workers and Alternative Dispute Resolution* (Washington, DC: National Association of Social Workers, 2014), 7.

14 Shapiro, *Courts*, 1, 3.

15 Roberts, *Order and Dispute*, 97.

16 Richard Borshay Lee, *The !Kung San: Men, Women, and Work in a Foraging Society* (Cambridge: Cambridge University Press, 1979), 370–398; Roberts, *Order and Dispute*, 84. Jealousy was the prime cause of discord. Elizabeth Marshall Thomas,

ical for hunter-gatherer societies,[17] such as the Eskimos[18] and the Andaman Islanders.[19] These might be considered active forms of lumping it.

In some other foraging societies, including some in Australia, avoidance or exile are possible outcomes of formal disputing processes. "Hunter-gatherer societies have friendly peacemakers, but owing to their largely egalitarian social organization, they tend not to rely significantly on mediators . . ."[20] Stanley Diamond refers to "a historically profound distinction between crime and certain types of violence. In primitive societies violence tends to be personally structured, nondissociative and, thereby, self-limiting."[21]

Studies of the social primates (which is all of them) show that they, too, have dispute resolution practices. Fights are common, but, as among foragers, bystanders often break up the fight, which is usually soon followed by reconciliation. As among us humans, after couples quarrel, they often reconcile by having sex.[22] That is a bilateral dispute resolution mechanism. There are other such bilateral mechanisms, where reconciliation is effected, when it is, by mutual behavior. Reconciliation procedures have been identified in at least 25 non-human primate societies.[23] What I find most interesting is that

---

The Old Way: A Story of the First People (New York: Farrar Straus Giroux, 2006), 169–70. The San "distinguish three levels of conflict: talking, fighting and deadly fighting [using deadly weapons]. . . . At each stage attempts are made to dampen the conflict and prevent it from escalating to the next level." Richard B. Lee, *The Dobe Ju/'hansi* (2nd ed.; Fort Worth, TX: Harcourt College Publishers), 97.

17 Black, "Elementary Forms of Conflict Management," 80.

18 Asen Balici, *The Netsilik Eskimo* (Garden City, NY: Natural History Press, 1970), 192–93.

19 Lidio Cipriani, *The Andaman Islanders*, ed. & trans. D. Taylor Fox (New York & Washington, DC: Frederick A. Praeger, 1966), 43.

20 Douglas P. Fry, "Conflict Management in Cross-Cultural Perspective," in *Natural Conflict Resolution*, ed. Filippo Aureli & Frans de Waal (Berkeley, CA: University of California Press, 2000), 336.

21 Diamond, *In Search of the Primitive*, 368–69 n. 50.

22 Frans de Waal, *Peacemaking among Primates* (Cambridge: Harvard University Press, 1989), 206.

23 *Natural Conflict Resolution*, Appendix A, "The Occurrence of Reconciliation in

some primates have third-party dispute resolution procedures (chimpanzees, for instance, have mediation)[24] despite the fact that the animals lack language, although they don't lack other ways of communicating with each other.

In more complex class societies, avoidance (or, from organizations: "exit"[25]) is also common. Thus American suburbia has been called an "avoidance culture."[26] But in modern urban society, avoidance can be more difficult. Battered wives, for instance, are not always in a position to move out. And avoidance, even where practicable, may be just bowing to superior force. The absence of a formalized dispute resolution process is arguably why the Kalahari Bushmen, when studied in the 1960s, had an even higher homicide rate than the United States at that time.[27] One ethnographer described a New Guinea society where, in his opinion, the absence of third-party dispute resolution processes accounted for why a dispute over a pig could escalate into a war.[28] Nonetheless, some primitive societies, which lack even these mechanisms, are reasonably orderly and peaceful.[29]

In arbitration, the parties (or the plaintiff) empower a third party to hand down an authoritative decision, as a judge does.[30]

Nonhuman Primates," 383.

24 De Waal, *Peacemaking*, 241–42.

25 Black, "The Elementary Forms of Conflict Management," 80; Albert O. Hirschman, *Exit, Voice, and Loyalty: Responses to Decline in Firms, Organizations, and States* (Cambridge: Harvard University Press, 1970), ch. 3 & *passim*.

26 Baumgartner, *Moral Order of a Suburb*, ch. 3.

27 Lee, *The !Kung San*, 398.

28 Klaus-Friedrich Koch, "Pigs and Politics in the New Guinea Highlands," in Nader & Todd, *Disputing Process*, 41–58. The article is adapted from Klaus-Friedrich Koch, *War and Peace in Jalémó: The Management of Conflict in Highland New Guinea* (Cambridge: Harvard University Press, 1974). Curiously, the famous McHoy/Hatfield feud also originated in a dispute over a pig. Black, "'Wild Justice,'" 252 & n. 45; Alina L. Walker, *Feud: Hatfields, McCoys, and Social Change in Appalachia, 1860–1900* (London & Chapel Hill, NC: University of North Carolina Press, 1988), 2–3.

29 Roberts, *Order and Dispute*, 158.

30 Sarah Rudolph Cole & Kristen M. Blankley, "Arbitration," in *The Handbook of Dispute Resolution*, ed. Michael L. Moffitt & Robert C. Bordone (San Francisco, CA: Jossey-Bass, 2005), 318–19; Roberts, *Order and Dispute*, 70–71, 135.

It's not mediation: "Mediation and arbitration have conceptually nothing in common. The one involves helping people to decide for themselves; the other involves helping people by deciding for them."[31]

But arbitration is not quite adjudication either, because of several differences. In adjudication, the decision-maker is an official, an officeholder who is not chosen by the parties. There, the third party (the judge) decides according to law—a law which is not of the parties' own making and which is not, for them, a matter of choice. In the United States, some business contracts and many labor/management collective bargaining agreements provide for arbitration. Arbitrators are usually drawn from a body of trained experts, the American Arbitration Association, which is a membership organization with codes of professional standards.[32] Often the arbitrator has some expertise in the industry.[33] The arbitrator interprets and enforces a law which the parties have previously made for themselves.

Because arbitration is coercive in its result, and better for those with more power than for those with less, many businesses have incorporated mandatory arbitration clauses into consumer contracts so as to restrict consumer remedies and keep consumers out of the courts.[34] One federal circuit court held that such contracts are unconscionable and therefore illegal.[35] The problem became so serious that many congressional

---

31 A.S. Meyer, "Functions of the Mediator in Collective Bargaining," Industrial & Labor Relations Rev. 13 (1960), 164. "However the two processes have a way of shading into each other." Ibid.

32 *Social Workers and Alternative Dispute Resolution*, 4–5; American Arbitration Association, "The Code of Ethics for Arbitration in Commercial Disputes," May 1, 2004, & idem; "Code of Professional Responsibility for Arbitrators of Labor Management Disputes," Sept. 2007, at htpps://www.adr.org.

33 Carrie Menkel-Meadow, "Roots and Inspirations: A Brief History of the Foundations of Dispute Resolution," in *Handbook of Dispute Resolution*, 318.

34 *Social Workers and Alternative Dispute Resolution*, 5; Michael L. Moffitt & Robert C. Bordone, "Perspectives on Dispute Resolution: An Introduction," *Handbook of Dispute Resolution*, 21.

35 *In re American Express Merchants' Litigation v. American Express*, 634 F.2d 182 (2d Cir. 2011).

hearings were held.[36] Nothing resulted. In 2010, the U.S. Supreme Court upheld consumer arbitration clauses which preclude judicial review.[37] As a (predictable) result, "few plaintiffs pursue low-value claims and super repeat-players [big business] perform particularly well."[38]

Sooner or later, Alternative Dispute Resolution (ADL) is always co-opted. Usually sooner.

However, in primitive societies, arbitration is rare,[39] so I will not be discussing it any further. If anarchists ever bother to think about such things, they might consider whether there's a place for arbitration in their blueprints for the future. The more complex, hierarchic and coercive their societies may be, the better suited they would be to compulsory arbitration: bringing the state back in, on the sly. I am thinking, in particular, of anarcho-syndicalism.

In adjudication, a dispute—a "case"—is initiated by a complainant in court. In criminal cases, the complainant is the state, not a private party, but for present purposes, the difference from civil cases doesn't matter. The court is a previously constituted, standing tribunal. Court proceedings are initiated voluntarily by a public official or a private party, but after that, although the litigants still make some choices, they are subject

---

36 Mandatory Binding Arbitration Agreements: Are They Fair for Consumers? hearing before the Subcommittee on Commercial and Administrative Law of the Committee on the Judiciary, House of Representatives, 110th Cong., 1st sess., June 12, 2007; Federal Arbitration Act: Is the Credit Card Industry Using It to Quash Legal Claims? hearing before the Subcommittee on Commercial and Administrative Law of the Committee on the Judiciary, House of Representatives, 111th Cong., 1st sess., May 5, 2009; Arbitration or Arbitrary: The Misuse of Mandatory Arbitration to Collect Consumer Debts: hearing before the Subcommittee on Domestic Policy of the Committee on Oversight and Governmental Reform, House of Representatives, 111th Cong., 1st sess., July 22, 2009; Mandatory Binding Arbitration: Is It Fair and Voluntary? hearing before the Subcommittee on Commercial and Administrative Law of the Committee on the Judiciary, House of Representatives, 111th Cong., 1st sess., Sept. 15, 2009; Arbitration: Is it Fair When Forced? hearing before the Committee on the Judiciary, U.S. Senate, 112th Cong., 1st sess., Oct. 13, 2011.

37 *Rent-a-Center West, Inc. v. Jackson*, 561 U.S. 63, 72 (2010). "Rent-to-own" is one of the worst rackets for exploiting low-income consumers.

38 David Horton & Andrea Camm Chandrasekher, "After the Revolution: An Empirical Study of Consumer Arbitration," *Georgetown L.J.* 104(1) (Nov. 2015), 124.

39 Roberts, *Order and Dispute*, 163–64.

to pre-existing rules of procedure and the decisions of the judge. They are always subject to the pre-existing laws of the state.[40]

Characteristic features of adjudication as an ideal stress "the use of a third party with coercive power, the usually 'win or lose' nature of the decision, and the tendency of the decision to focus narrowly on the immediate matter in issue as distinguished from a concern with the underlying relationship between the parties."[41] In short: "Judges do not merely give opinions; they give orders."[42]

In adjudication (litigation) the case is decided by a judge who doesn't know the parties. He doesn't care about the background of the dispute. He is not interested in repairing the relationship between the parties, if they had or have one. He is not supposed to consider those matters. The judge should be impartial and disinterested, deciding the cases on the basis of the parties presenting "proofs and reasoned arguments."[43] His decision "must rest solely on the legal rules and evidence adduced at the hearing."[44] Rules of evidence, which are more numerous and complex in the United States than in any other legal system, narrowly circumscribe the admission of evidence, especially at trial. Resolutions of cases arising from interpersonal disputes are "constrained in their scope of inquiry by rules of evidence . . ."[45] U.S. courts are designedly better, in the terminology of Donald L. Horowitz, at identifying the "historical facts" of the particular case (whodunit) than the "social facts" which might be illustrative of the general circumstances

---

[40] Felsteiner, "Influences of Social Organization on Dispute Processing," 48; Kenneth I. Winston, "Introduction," *The Principles of Social Order*, 28–29.

[41] Sander, "Varieties of Dispute Processing," 28.

[42] Black, "Toward a Theory of the Third Party," *Social Organization of Right and Wrong*, 114.

[43] Fuller, "The Forms and Limits of Adjudication," *Principles of Social Order*, 93–94.

[44] *Goldberg v. Kelly*, 397 U.S. 254, 271 (1969).

[45] Robert C. Davis, "Mediation: The Brooklyn Experiment," *Neighborhood Justice*, 156.

which regularly give rise to cases like the one at bar.[46]

That doesn't mean that courts are very good at that either. Poverty is never put on trial; poor people are put on trial. But the courts, despite the title of a book by a reform-minded judge,[47] are never on trial. It isn't difficult to show that the ideal of the rule of law, thus institutionalized, is a failure even on its own terms. Anarchists and others have shown that repeatedly.

My first topic is mediation as practiced in more or less primitive societies, and its implications for contemporary anarchism. I emphasize that mediation is voluntary. The parties choose to submit their dispute to a mediator, not for a ruling, but for help. They, or sometimes just the complainant, may select the mediator, or he might be "appointed by someone in authority, [but] both principals must agree to his intervention."[48]

Mediation is not primarily concerned with enforcing rules, although the parties may cite rules to support their positions. In mediation, unlike adjudication, there is no such thing as irrelevant or inadmissible evidence.[49] People may talk themselves out. The purpose of mediation is not to identify who is to blame, although the parties will do lots of blaming. The purpose of mediation is rather to solve an interpersonal problem which, unresolved, will probably become a social problem.

The forms of dispute resolution I am describing are ideal types. One legal philosopher, Lon L. Fuller, insists that they should be kept distinct because each has its own "morality." Often in reality they are not so pure (such as in the Ifugao example which follows, which Fuller was accordingly unable

---

46 Donald L. Horowitz, *The Courts and Social Policy* (Washington, DC: The Brookings Institution, 1977), 45, 48. Whether they are very good at ascertaining even historical facts is a topic which, to my knowledge, has never been investigated.

47 Jerome Frank, *Courts on Trial: Myth and Reality in American Justice* (New York: Atheneum, 1963) (originally 1949).

48 Nader & Todd, "Introduction," 10.

49 *E.g.*, James L. Gibbs, Jr., "The Kpelle Moot," in *Law and Warfare: Studies in the Anthropology of Conflict,* ed. Paul Bohannan (Garden City, NY: The American Museum of Natural History, 1967), 282–83.

to understand[50]). Even the distinction between voluntary and involuntary processes, which I consider so important, is often not a bright-line distinction. Power is insinuated into many relationships which are not officially or overtly coercive.[51] If consent can be a matter of degree, nonetheless, one may ask "what proportion of nonconsensuality is implied in such a power relation, and whether that degree of nonconsensuality is necessary or not, and then one may question every power relation to that extent."[52]

This, however, seems to be universally true: "Adjudication and mediation are in principle opposites, and can be separated analytically. But they do not represent *historical* oppositions": "There are societies in the world ... without formal procedures for judgement, but there are none without legitimate procedures for mediation."[53]

One inevitable consequence of involving a third party is that a third party always has his own agenda.[54] That is not necessarily a bad thing. American arbitrators of business/business and labor/management disputes are chosen and paid by the disputants, and they might lose *their* business if they are perceived to be biased or—so to speak—arbitrary. Elsewhere, the

---

50 "What appear to us [sic] as hopelessly confusing ambiguities of role were probably not perceived as such either by the occupant of the role [the mediator, the *monkulun*] or by those subject to his ministrations." [Fuller,] "Mediation—Its Forms and Functions," 156. Of course Fuller is hopelessly confused when he looks for his Platonic Forms and finds only reality. Laura Nader's work in a Mexican town "illustrates how a single person, the president, may be mediator, adjudicator, and arbitrator all in one day." Nader & Todd, "Introduction," 10; see Laura Nadar, *Harmony Ideology: Justice and Control in a Zapotec Mountain Village* (Stanford, CA: Stanford University Press, 1990), 122. There's a lot of evidence from many times and places of judges acting as conciliators or arbitrators. *E.g.*, Nicole Castan, "The Arbitration of Disputes Under the 'Ancien Regime,'" in *Disputes and Settlements,* 259–60. The "style" of adjudication may be penal, compensatory, therapeutic, or conciliatory. Donald Black, *The Behavior of Law* (New York: Academic Press, 1976), 4–5.

51 Michel Foucault, "Truth and Power," *The Foucault Reader*, ed. Paul Rabinow (New York: Pantheon Books, 1984), 61.

52 Foucault, "Politics and Ethics: An Interview," in ibid., 379.

53 *The Settlement of Disputes in Early Medieval Europe*, "Conclusion," 237. The Conclusion is unsigned.

54 Gulliver, "On Mediators," 16.

third party facilitator might be a socially prominent tribal mediator who strives to build a reputation as a successful problem-solver (bringing in more mediation business—for which he, too, is paid[55]). Or he might be an American judge looking to be re-elected, or aspiring to higher office.

Undoubtedly "every process, every institution has its characteristic ways of operating; each is biased toward certain types of outcomes; each leaves its distinctive imprint on the matters it touches."[56] Third-party dispute deciders or resolvers are usually of higher social status than the disputants.[57] That may be

---

55 Barton, *Ifugao Law*, 87, 88–89.

56 Horowitz, *The Courts and Social Policy*, 24.

57 "Friendly peacemakers tend to be about equal to the adversaries, whereas mediators, arbitrators, and adjudicators tend to be (in the same order) increasingly elevated above the adversaries." Black, "Elementary Forms of Conflict Management," 86.

This issue came up after I delivered, as a speech, in Manila, a version of this article. One of the formal responders gave his own speech in praise of the Katarungang Bambarangay (or Barangay Justice System) in the Philippines. It provides, on a neighborhood or village basis, for compulsory "mediation" of certain kinds of disputes between residents of the same barangay (the smallest unit of government, typically corresponding to a rural village or an urban neighborhood). The mediators consist of a barangay "captain," an elected official, in association with conciliation committees of local residents. The system remotely resembles some earlier indigenous dispute resolution institutions, such as that of the Ifugao. From the little I know of them, they may not have some of the defects which vitiated our Neighborhood Justice Centers (*infra*). The barangays are much smaller, and probably more homogeneous than the catchment areas of the NJCs. This system probably moves faster than the regular courts, and lawyers are not necessary—in fact, they are banned. It has reliable permanent financing from the national government. In the United States, parties to lawsuits, or involved in criminal prosecutions, may feel like the proceedings are conducted in a foreign language. In the Philippines, they actually are. In the regular courts, proceedings are conducted in English, and the English language proficiency of Filipinos, as I learned during a 17-day visit, varies widely. In the barangay courts, the local language is used.

The system was initiated in 1975, by Presidential Decree No. 1508—by President Ferdinand Marcos, who had assumed dictatorial power and imposed martial law. He had political reasons for doing that. Nonetheless, in three villages in Cebu Province, the rural population in the 1970's accepted the system as useful for them. G. Sidney Silliman, "A Political Analysis of the Philippines' Katarungang Pambarangay System of Informal Justice Through Mediation," *Law & Soc'y Rev.* 19(2) (1985): 279–302. Obviously I lack up-to-date sources. But it is at least clear that this system of informal justice is not, as it has been called, a non-state justice system. S. Golub, "Non-State Justice Systems in Bangladesh and the Philippines" (2003), Department for International Development (London), http://www.gsdrc.org/go/display/document/legacyid/825.

Through its "Rule of Law Initiative," the American Bar Association is promoting

essential to their effectiveness: they have to be taken seriously. Obviously, mediation on these terms may not be something to be imported, as-is and unthinkingly, into a neo-anarchist society. But unless it can be imported thinkingly, into an egalitarian society which not only tolerates, but encourages excellence—and therefore a measure of inequality—mediation will never be as effective as it could be.

---

the barangay courts with the same uncritical self-satisfaction it brought to promoting Neighborhood Justice Centers and Restorative Justice (discussed herein) in the United States. "Small Claims Courts and Barangay Justice Advocates Collaborate to Resolve Disputes" (Oct. 2010), http://www.americanbar.org/rule_of_law.

2. Case Studies

LET'S LOOK AT TWO EXAMPLES from the ethnographic literature.

1. THE PLATEAU TONGA

I begin with a true story about a conflict which arose among the Plateau Tonga[1] of what is now Zambia. Traditionally they were shifting cultivators and herdsmen. In 1948, they were a dispersed, partly dispossessed and rather demoralized population of farmers and herders. Europeans had taken some of their best land. At a beer party, Mr. A, who was drunk, slugged Mr. B. These men belonged to different clans and lived in different villages. Unexpectedly, and unfortunately, after several days, Mr. B died.

This was a stateless society. But there were social groups whose interests were directly affected by this homicide. The Tonga are matrilineal. For most purposes, a person's most important affiliation is with a limited number of matrilineal relatives. This is the group which receives bridewealth when its women marry, and it's the group which inherits most of

---

[1] I will usually not provide detailed page citations to ethnographic sources. For the Plateau Tonga, my sources are: E. Colson, "Social Control and Vengeance in Plateau Tonga Society"; Elizabeth Colson, *The Plateau Tonga of Northern Rhodesia: Social and Religious Studies* (Manchester, England: Manchester University Press, 1962) (the "Social Control" article is chapter 3, at 102–121); Elizabeth Colson, "The Plateau Tonga of Northern Rhodesia," in *Seven Tribes of British Central Africa*, ed. Elizabeth Colson & Max Gluckman (Manchester, England: Manchester University Press, 1951), 94–162.

a man's property when he dies. It's also the group that's primarily responsible for paying compensation for the person's offences, and for exacting vengeance.

The *father's* matrilineal group (which, by definition, is different from the son's) is also an interested party. It is *also* liable for a member's offenses, but to a lesser extent, and it also inherits from him, although it gets a smaller share than the matrilineal kin-group. By killing Mr. B, Mr. A did an injury to Mr. B's group. For several reasons, Mr. B's group didn't take vengeance on Mr. A or, if they couldn't get at him, against one of his relatives. If it did, a blood feud would result, with back and forth killings until everybody got sick of it. Another reason for not taking vengeance is that the British-imposed court system would have arrested the avenger. (Mr. A himself was in fact arrested, convicted of manslaughter, and sent to prison,[2] but that didn't square things between the kin groups; Mr. B's group had lost a member, and it demanded compensation.)

The kin groups were intermarried. They also lived among one another. The Tonga lived in very small villages of about 100 people. Most villagers were not members of the same core kin group. But their fellow villagers were their neighbors and some of their friends, and they were some of the people they worked with. The villagers, as neighbors, also had an interest in a peaceful resolution of the dispute.

Before Mr. B died, the A group had made apologetic and conciliatory overtures to the B group. But after he died, all communication ceased. The matter had become too serious. This caused a lot of trouble for many people, especially if they

---

2 This example, and all the others I discuss, are based on observations of peoples subject to Western colonialism. Elizabeth Colson was an employee of the British colonial regime. The dispute processing institutions all existed by the recognition or sufferance of the colonial powers, which created formal court systems for what they considered serious crimes and claims. The indigenous disputing processes were, therefore, subordinate parts of what are now called "dual" legal systems. However, their subordinate position did not detract from the fact that, within the jurisdiction allowed to them, they generally worked. As Colson writes, "These [traditional forms] still work to reach a settlement over and above that which can be obtained through the courts. They are interested, not in the punishment of the offenders, but in the re-establishment of good relations between the groups involved." Colson, "Social Control and Vengeance," 204.

had ties to both groups. Ordinary social life was disrupted. Even husbands and wives might stop speaking to each other, because they were often related to different, and now hostile, kin groups. Something had to be done.

Mr. C, a prominent member of A's group, found a go-between who was related by marriage to both groups. All along, B's group admitted that Mr. B was obviously the wrongdoer. He had a reputation as a troublemaker. Nobody was sorry when he went to prison. B's group's concern was over how much compensation it would have to pay. The case had to end with payment of compensation. A feud was inconceivable, because so many people in each group were related to people in the other group, and the groups were intermarried. It was these cross-cutting ties that made everybody want a generally acceptable settlement. In modern societies, usually these ties don't exist.

The anthropologist, Elizabeth Colson, doesn't report the specifics of the settlement. Because they don't matter. She wrote an article about this because she'd published a general account of Plateau Tonga society, and some of her readers just couldn't understand how there could be anything but anarchy under a system of, well, *anarchy*.[3]

2. The Ifugao

About 35 years earlier, the situation would have been dealt with in a somewhat different way by the Ifugao[4] of northern Luzon. They were stateless, pagan wet-rice cultivators. And headhunters. They were anarchists too, but their society was more stratified than the Tonga society. An American, Roy Barton, taught

---

3 Colson, "Social Control," 199–200, 210–211.

4 Barton, *Ifugao Law*; R.W. Barton, *Autobiographies of Three Pagans in the Philippines* (New Hyde Park, NY: University Books, 1963) (originally 1938); R.W. Barton, *The Half-Way Sun* (New York: Brewer & Warren, 1930); R.W. Barton, *The Kalingas: Their Institutions and Customary Law* (Chicago, IL: University of Chicago Press, 1949) (not primarily about the Ifugao, but with frequent comparisons to them); E. Adamson Hoebel, *The Law of Primitive Man: A Study in Comparative Legal Dynamics* (Cambridge & London: Harvard University Press, 2006), ch. 6 (originally 1954).

school there from 1906 to 1917. His predecessor had been speared. He learned the language and wrote a well-respected book on Ifugao law. I'll be speaking in the present tense (what anthropologists call "the ethnographic present"), but the story is based on evidence of practices in the period before 1903, before American authority became effective in the highlands. Spanish authority had never been effective in the highlands.

Let's assume the same situation as among the Tonga: an unintentional killing by a drunken man. Drunken brawls among young men occurred among the Ifugao too. If the killing had been intentional, the kin group of the victim would have killed the wrongdoer.[5] If they couldn't get at the wrongdoer himself, they would kill one of his relatives. The result, in either event, is a blood feud. A death for a death, until the groups get sick of it. But an unintentional killing by a drunk would usually be resolved by mediation resulting in the payment of compensation by the one kin group to the other.

The aggrieved party, or in this case one of his relatives, initiates the process. The plaintiff would recruit a go-between, known as a *mankulun*. The only restriction is that the mediator not be closely related to either party. The mediator would be a relatively wealthy man, and usually a successful headhunter. He was preferably somebody with experience mediating disputes. He could also recruit more support from relatives and dependents than most people could do. If he arranges a settlement, he is paid a fee by the defendant, and his prestige is enhanced. And like everybody else, he wants the matter to be settled peacefully.

In theory, the defendant is free to reject mediation. In practice, the *mankulun* makes him an offer he can't refuse. If the defendant won't listen to him, "the *monkalun* waits until he

---

[5] Barton states as the general rule that unintentional homicides are compensable, but, that is at the option of the victim's kin. One of his informants insisted that if a hunter through carelessness in handling his spear caused a death, that would not be compensable. Barton, *Autobiography*, 182. That may reflect a local variation in the law, or, it occurs to me, a distinction between an innocent and a negligent homicide. Ifugaos consider a drunk not to be blameworthy. In U.S. law, voluntary intoxication mitigates but does not excuse a homicide.

ascends into his house, follows him, and, war-knife in hand, sits in front of him and compels him to listen." The defendant is well aware that the mediator has used knives—maybe this very knife—to cut off heads. He accepts mediation.[6]

Once that happens, the parties and their relatives are forbidden to talk to each other. Whatever they have to say to each other, has to go through the *mankalun*, even if it has nothing to do with the dispute. I think this is very ingenious. It keeps the parties from getting into angry arguments and making matters worse. It makes it possible for the mediator to manipulate everybody for their own good. The conflict imposes a social cost on the village, because it disrupts the ordinary social relations and the economic cooperation among members of the kin groups, as it did among the Plateau Tonga. So it's in the interest of a lot of the local people to have the case resolved.

Formal separation of the parties is not a typical feature of mediation in primitive societies.[7] But in all societies where mediators operate, the mediator's shuttle diplomacy results in a de facto cooling-off period. In early medieval Ireland, there were dispute resolution practices which proceeded by stages, with, in between them, "a formal 'cooling off period' to prevent a dispute from getting out of control, and to allow maximum opportunity for private agreement" before a defendant's intransigence led to "independent adjudication."[8] Courtroom "delay" in the United States is widely decried, but it may serve the same function.

Occasionally U.S. law provides for cooling off periods during the processing of disputes. Under the Railway Labor Act, in case of disputes between management and labor, when

---

[6] "The word *monkalun* comes from the root *kalun*, meaning *advise*. The Ifugao word has the double sense, too, of our word *advise*, as used in the following sentences, 'I have the honor to advise you of your appointment!' and 'I advise you not to do that.'" Barton, *Ifugao Law*, 87 n. 19.

[7] P.H. Gulliver, "On Mediators," in *Social Anthropology and Law*, ed. Ian Hamnett (London: Academic Press, 1977), 33.

[8] Richard Sharpe, "Dispute Settlement in Medieval Ireland," in *The Settlement of Disputes in Early Medieval Europe*, 180–81.

the parties remain at an impasse despite mediation, the National Mediation Board mediator orders a 30-day cooling off period during which the parties may continue to negotiate or agree to arbitration, but with the stipulation that they cannot resort to self-help (such as strikes and lockouts). Thereafter, the cooling off period may be extended indefinitely if a presidential emergency board is created to formulate recommendations. If these are refused, a final 30-day cooling off period begins to run.[9]

One group of people who especially desire a settlement is people who are related to both parties. The closest kin really do have to side with their kinsman, although they don't have to like it. But those who aren't so closely related to one side will be severely criticized if they take sides in the dispute. They want a settlement on almost any terms.

The mediator is a go-between. But he's not just relaying messages. He actively shapes the settlement as it eventually emerges. Mediators almost always do that. I'll quote from Barton again, because this quotation often appears in books about the anthropology of law:

> To the end of peaceful settlement, he exhausts every art of Ifugao diplomacy. He wheedles, coaxes, flatters, threatens, drives, scolds, insinuates. He beats down the demands of the plaintiff or prosecution, and bolsters up the proposals of the defendants until a point be reached at which the two parties may compromise.

It's part of the game that the defendant initially refuses a settlement offer. These are proud people. Even a defendant who is obviously in the wrong is expected to be truculent for a while.[10] He's saving face. These are my kind of people.

---

9 45 U.S.C. §§ 151–164, 181–188.

10 This was also true of 16th-century Scotland. The problem was that in an honor society no one wanted to appear to be too keen to compromise. More commonly, therefore, the initiative for that peace came from kinsmen, friends, and neighbors who were concerned that the feud was disrupting the locality. Keith M. Brown, *Bloodfeud in Scotland, 1573–1625: Violence, Justice and Politics in an Early Modern Society* (Edinburgh, Scotland: John Donald Publishers Ltd., 1986), 45. Feud was, at this time,

In another society, "Even where a principal's claim is very strong and the balance of bargaining power lies with him, he commonly makes some effort to show tolerance and good will by giving way to his opponent in at least some small degree."[11] He makes some token concession.

However, if the mediator thinks that the defendant is being unreasonable for too long, he may formally withdraw from the case. For the next two weeks, the parties and their kin can't engage in hostilities. After the truce expires, retaliation, which may include revenge killings, commences. Nobody wants that. Usually the defendant backs down. But not always. It's possible to start over with a new mediator. But this won't go on endlessly. In another book, Ralph Barton mentions a case where the defendant deserted his wife and refused to pay compensation to her kinsmen. He rejected the settlements negotiated by *four* mediators. The plaintiff's kin then speared him. The defendant's family didn't do anything about it.[12]

This is not the only way the Ifugaos coped with conflicts, or failed to. A serious crime among family intimates (such as theft, or even homicide, between brothers) is likely to go unpunished. Disputes are between, not within, groups. A group can't punish itself or claim compensation from itself. This is also the situation in some other primitive societies. But it is also true that in legally ordered state societies, law is least effective in regulating intimate relationships, those among people with the least "relational difference."[13]

The Ifugao mediation procedure which I've described is also increasingly inactive as the relational difference among the disputants increases beyond local, more or less face to face social networks so as to implicate people who are more

---

common to Highland and Lowland Scotland. Jenny Wormald, "The Blood Feud in Early Modern Scotland," in *Disputes and Settlements*, 105–06.

11 P.H. Gulliver, "Dispute Settlement Without Courts: The Ndeneuli of Southern Tanzania," in *Law in Culture and Society*, ed. Laura Nadar (Berkeley, CA: University of California Press, 1997), 67 (originally 1969).

12 Hoebel, *The Law of Primitive Man*, 110–111.

13 Black, *Behavior of Law*, 40–41.

distant socially and geographically. Ralph Barton described the Ifugaos—who were not an especially peaceable people—as occupying concentric "war zones" radiating outwards. As disputes crossed the borders of zones, they became more serious, and more likely to be resolved by violence. In the outermost zone, the word "dispute" hardly applies. There, anybody you don't know is an enemy, to be killed on sight. There is no doubt that primitive societies in general have often failed to establish mechanisms for the resolution of intergroup conflicts the more closely the situation approximates war.

But again, this is where states have also conspicuously failed, despite the United Nations, "international law," etc. They often lack the common ground, the middle ground on which to base resolutions of disputes. We are at our worst at solving our problems when we are either too close, or too far apart. "The relationship between law and relational distance is curvilinear": "Law is inactive among intimates, increasing as the distance between people increases but decreasing as this reaches a point at which people live in entirely separate worlds."[14] "This double conception of morality," wrote Kropotkin, in tranquil late Victorian England, "passes through the whole evolution of mankind, and maintains itself now." He added that if Europeans had in some measure "extended our *ideas* of solidarity—in theory at least—over the nation, and partly over other nations as well—we have lessened the *bonds* of solidarity within our own nations, and even within our own families."[15] In 1914, like many other thoughtful people, he was shocked to discover how tenuous international solidarity really was.

---

14 Black, *Behavior of Law*, 41 (emphasis deleted).

15 Peter Kropotkin, *Mutual Aid: A Factor of Evolution* (Boston, MA: Extending Horizons Books, 1960), 113 (emphasis added) (originally published 1902). I would like to thank Michael Disnevic (letter to Bob Black, March 3, 2016) for reminding me to re-view this book. Kropotkin held the curious belief that international law, because it is customary law (which is not entirely true), embodies values of mutual aid and equality. Peter Kropotkin, "A New Work on International Law," *The Speaker* (April 1, 1905), 7–8.

In my title I use the word "justice." I was thinking, not of justice as a moral value, but of justice (as in the phrase "criminal justice") as a social institution. Ever since Plato's *Republic*, philosophers, in trying to explicate justice as a value, have often, instead of defining it, described "just" institutions. In modern political philosophy, probably the most influential theory of justice, and certainly the most famous, is that of John Rawls. But Rawls' articulation of "justice as fairness" is not about fairness among individuals, but rather fairness as a measure of a just political society.[16] For Rawls, justice means social justice.[17] Rawls had nothing to say about the just resolution of interpersonal disputes, although that is the first and usually the only thing that most people think of when they think of justice. Post-Rawls philosophers such as Jeremy Waldron think of justice in terms of "neutrality," not a word Rawls originally emphasized.[18] For Waldron the word does apply, even if not exclusively, to third-party dispute resolution: "The neutrality of the third party is a matter of his relation to the contest between the other two."[19] The emphasis is on the third party's impartiality. That is what makes his decision fair.

But, does it? Is it even fairness we are looking at—or looking for—in "justice, primitive"? The Ifugao mediator is not neutral. He is not impartial. He is partial toward both parties. He is partial to society. He is partial toward himself. He is not a judge. He is not deciding which party is right and which party is wrong. He is not deciding anything. He is trying to resolve a problem between two disputants which implicate the interests of other people too. He isn't even trying to be "fair." Whatever its other merits, compromise is unfair where the fault is entirely on one side. But mediated outcomes are always compromises.

---

16 John Rawls, *Justice as Fairness: A Restatement*, ed. Erin Kelly (Cambridge: Belknap Press of Harvard University Press, 2001); idem, *A Theory of Justice* (Cambridge: Harvard University Press, 1971), 3 ("Justice is the first virtue of social institutions, as truth is of systems of thought").

17 Ibid., 54.

18 Jeremy Waldron, "Legislation and Moral Neutrality," *Liberal Rights: Collected Papers, 1981–1991* (Cambridge: Cambridge University Press, 1993), 144–45.

19 Ibid., 145.

I see two ways to characterize the mediator's activity with respect to justice as fairness. One way is that mediation working toward reconciliation or pacification is another, better kind of justice. The other way is that whatever mediation accomplishes, when it succeeds, is something better than justice. For me, as an anarchist, peace and freedom are more important than justice. I think that justice will be a byproduct of freedom more often than freedom will be a byproduct of justice.

3. Multiplex Relationships

Now I will get a bit theoretical. There's something about these disputes that makes them different from many disputes in modern societies. In a modern urban society a dispute usually involves only one social relationship between the parties, and it is often the case that there is no social relationship. Each party plays a single role. Your landlord probably doesn't also know you through interactions at church or in a common workplace, and your employer isn't likely to be your relative (except in the Philippines). They are not your friends. The anthropologist Max Gluckman calls these relationships *simplex relationships*.[1] American suburbanites, for example, share few ties, and "even while they exist, most suburban relationships encompass only a few strands of people's lives."[2]

Just as an individual may have multiple relations with someone else, he may have relationships with people who have relationships with each other. Describing a Mexican Indian town, Laura Nader writes: "Cross-linkage brings a number of individuals or groups together, while dividing them by linking certain members with different groups. The degree to which

---

[1] Max Gluckman, *The Ideas in Barotse Jurisprudence* (2nd ed.; New Haven, CT & London: Yale University Press, 1967), 19–20; Max Gluckman, *The Judicial Process Among the Barotse of Northern Rhodesia* (Manchester, England, UK: Manchester University Press, 1965), 5–6.

[2] "Such ties usually arise from residential proximity or common membership in an organization, and they are only rarely buttressed by shared employment, joint ownership of possessions, participation in a closed social network, or economic interdependence." Baumgartner, *Moral Order of a Suburb*, 9.

inter-group relations cross-link affects the development of balanced oppositions or factions in the town."[3] Those who have ties to both parties to a dispute have a personal interest, in addition to the general interest, in the harmonious settlement of the dispute. Cross-links had a pacifying influence among the Plateau Tonga.[4]

In primitive societies, which are anarchist societies, if you get into a dispute with someone, he might be playing multiple roles in your life. Someone may be at the same time your brother-in-law, your creditor, your workmate and your neighbor. This is someone you probably encounter often in your everyday life. These multiple roles may multiply occasions for conflict, but they also motivate both of you resolve the conflict, because all these relationships taken together are probably more important than whatever the dispute is about. And there are typically a lot of other people who have an interest in a peaceful settlement. This is what Gluckman calls a *multiplex relationship*. He also argues that the more activities the disputants share, the more likely it is it for a dispute to be handled in a more conciliatory than authoritative fashion.[5]

There's a seeming paradox here. In complex societies, simplex relationships predominate. In simpler societies, multiplex relationships prevail. In Tonga and in Ifugao country, there were a lot of cross-links. There were many people with ties to both sides. And there was no state to impose law and order. Instead, the social organization provided very powerful inducements to make peace.

---

[3] Nader, *Harmony Ideology*, 36 (quoted), 274.

[4] Max Gluckman spoke of this as "the peace of the feud." *Custom and Conflict in Africa* (Oxford: Basil Blackwell, 1956), ch. 1. However, it doesn't always work out that way. Renato Rosaldo recounted a feud between two groups which was supplanted by their allying to raid a third group. *Ilongot Headhunting, 1883–1974: A Study in Society and History* (Stanford, CA: Stanford University Press, 1980), 273–74.

[5] Gluckman, *Judicial Process Among the Barotse of Northern Rhodesia,* 20–21.

4. Forms of Dispute Resolution

WHAT'S A DISPUTE? I'll adopt a definition used by some (not all) social scientists. A dispute begins with a grievance. Someone feels she has been wronged. She may complain to the wrongdoer. They might resolve the matter. Up to this point, it's been a completely private matter. But if they don't agree, and the victim goes public with the matter, then there's a dispute. Depending on the society, going public might mean calling the police, filing a lawsuit, or just complaining to people you know.

Negotiation is a two-party, bilateral form of dispute resolution. It probably exists everywhere. But it isn't the solution to every problem. A dyad can be deadlocked. Very often, as we saw, the involvement of a third party is helpful. My main objective here is to contrast mediation with adjudication. My focus is mediation. Mediation is appropriate to anarchist societies. You find adjudication usually in state societies. But it is questionable whether state societies are better served by adjudication than anarchist societies are served by mediation.

I will define mediation as a disputing process which is, above all, voluntary. It's one where the parties choose to submit a dispute to a mediator, not for a decision, but for help. It's not primarily concerned with enforcing rules, although the parties may invoke rules. The mediator's purpose isn't to identify somebody to blame, although the parties will do lots of blaming. The purpose is to solve a problem. This is an ideal type.

Ifugao mediation isn't quite pure, because it isn't commenced in a purely voluntary way. But it's much purer than what was later attempted in the name of mediation in the United States.

I will define adjudication as a process that results when a dispute—now known as a "case"—is initiated by a grievant in a court. A court is a permanent, pre-existing decisional tribunal. Its jurisdiction is compulsory. Cases are decided by a judge who doesn't know the parties. He isn't interested in repairing the relationship between the parties, if they have one. He doesn't care what the background of the dispute might be. He's not supposed to consider those things. He decides the case according to the laws of the state. Usually, if the case goes to trial, the judgment is that someone is "guilty" or not guilty of a crime, or that someone is or is not "at fault" in a civil case. Typically, one party wins and the other party loses. In mediation there aren't supposed to be any winners or losers, even if, viewed realistically, there are.

That's the ideal of adjudication. I could criticize it as a description of the American legal system, and, I suspect, every legal system. Adjudication doesn't even live up to its own ideal. But I don't even like the ideal version. Instead, I want to discuss what can happen when mediation is inserted into an adjudication system, supposedly as a legal reform.

5. The Politics of Informal Justice

A. *Solutions in Search of Problems*

In the 1960s, there was a tremendous amount of social and political conflict in the United States. Black people, women, poor people, students, prisoners, radicals and other people made demands on American society. By my definition, these were "disputes." The courts were recognizing many new rights. Alarmed lawyers spoke of a "rights revolution."

Now how did the legal establishment and the college professors react to this? They decided that the courts had heavy caseloads. The way to reduce their caseloads was by somehow preventing people from taking their supposedly minor disputes to court. As a point of fact, there is no evidence that most courts had heavy caseloads.[1] Many lawsuits were filed, but few of them come to trial. And Americans, who are supposedly so litigious, mostly go out of their way not to initiate litigation.

So, just when the downtrodden started to claim rights through adjudication, the legal establishment decided that we needed new, informal ways of rapidly processing the minor disputes of minor people.

There was nothing new about this ploy. Fifty years before, "small claims" courts were created to decide cases that were too small for lawyers to bother with. This was supposed to provide

---

1 Malcolm M. Feeley, *The Process Is the Punishment: Handling Cases in a Lower Criminal Court* (New York: Russell Sage Foundation, 1979), ch. 8. Federal courts, by now, may have heavy caseloads. But far more criminal and civil cases arise in state courts.

fast, inexpensive justice, without a lot of legal technicalities, usually without the involvement of lawyers. They called the small claims court the "people's court." The plaintiffs were supposed to be the humble people. But small claims court was really an eviction service for landlords and a collection agency for ghetto businesses. The people who were supposed to be the plaintiffs were usually the defendants.

So, in the 1980s, Richard Danzig, a scholar from the RAND Corporation,[2] proposed a new conflict resolution mechanism. He called for a "complementary, decentralized criminal justice system." By "complementary," he meant that it would be a supplement to the judicial system, not a replacement for it. He said that the new structures shouldn't be subordinated to the judicial system. But how could the systems co-exist unless one system was subordinated to the other? One or the other has to decide which system has jurisdiction over which cases. Obviously the courts would make that decision, because that's where cases start. The situation is analogous to "legal pluralism" under colonialism where the courts of the foreign, colonial regime adjudicate cases of serious crime and cases which directly implicate its interests, while the minor disputes (from the colonial power's perspective) among the natives are resolved, if they are, by indigenous dispute procedures.

Danzig's model was the system employed by the Kpelle in Liberia.[3] He called it a *moot*. He got this from an anthropologist named James L. Gibbs, Jr.[4] The word refers to Anglo-Saxon assemblies whose composition is somewhat uncertain and

---

2 He later became U.S. Secretary of the Navy—this was under President Bill Clinton. The U.S. military prefers unilateral, coercive dispute resolution. Danzig's wife is a psychotherapist.

3 The Kpelle made a previous appearance in my writings, for the way they organize and carry out work (they do not like hard work) in a relatively ludic way. Bob Black, "Primitive Affluence: A Postscript to Sahlins." *Friendly Fire* (Brooklyn, NY: Autonomedia, 1992), 30–31; Bob Black, *Instead of Work* (Berkeley, CA: LBC Books, 2015), 49–50. The former military dictator of Guinea, Moïse Dadis Camara, is a Kpelle. According to DNA testing, Oprah Winfrey is of Kpelle ancestry. She thought her ancestors were Zulus.

4 Gibbs, "The Kpelle Moot," 277–289.

whose function and procedures are totally unknown.[5] Gibbs described a relatively informal proceeding which was attended by the kinsmen and neighbors of the parties. The problem is usually a domestic issue. The assembly is held at the home of the complainant: home court advantage. Anybody can show up for it. The complainant appoints the so-called mediator, who is a socially important relative of his. That introduces bias right at the start. Apparently the procedure is compulsory for the defendant. The parties testify. They can cross-examine each other. They can cross-examine witnesses. A party might have some respected or articulate supporter speak for him. (I'd call that person a lawyer.) Anybody can speak, but the mediator can impose a token fine on somebody who, and I quote, "speaks out of turn." (The fine is standing for a round of drinks. Everybody is drinking at the "moot.") The mediator also says what *he* thinks about the case. Then he "expresses the consensus of the group." But he doesn't call for a vote. The audience does not deliberate. The consensus is whatever he says it is. The party who is mainly at fault is then required to formally apologize by providing token gifts to the wronged person. Then he has to provide beer or rum for everyone present.

This isn't mediation. It's adjudication with a biased judge who has more control over the temporary assembly than an American judge has over a temporary jury. It's court TV that isn't filmed. And it's a drinking party.

There is nothing resembling a moot in, for example, American suburbia.[6] How do you approximate this institution in a modern city? Here's an example from Danzig himself. Suppose that there's a juvenile loitering around outside a store:

> If the complaint [to the police] were replaced by a moot discussion, to which the teenager brought his friends, the shopkeeper and his associates (including his family, other

---

[5] The documentary sources "do not give any clue whatever to the nature and form"—or the functions and procedures—"of the assembly." George Laurence Gomme, *Primitive Folk-Moots; or, Open-Air Assemblies in Britain* (London: Sampson Low, Marston, Searle & Rivington, 1880), 50.

[6] Baumgartner, *Moral Order of a Suburb*, 41.

shopkeepers, his employees), *and* the police officers working with juveniles, there would be a fair chance for the kind of interchange which has proven valuable when staged as a one-event 'retreat' in other communities.[7]

If I were the teenager, I'd rather be arrested. Most of those other people have absolutely no reason to waste their time on a trivial problem that doesn't concern them. Yet these ideas would inspire, or justify anyway, the formation of federally funded Neighborhood Justice Centers, which don't even slightly resemble Danzig's idea of a moot, much less Gibbs' idea of a moot.

Boosters of the "neighborhood justice" model proudly recounted:

> Unlike small claims court and housing court, these programs are not watered-down versions of real courts. Their roots are not in Anglo-American jurisprudence, but in the African moots, in socialist comrades courts, in psychotherapy and in labor mediation.[8]

In point of fact, NJC mediation cases mostly originated as criminal prosecutions in ordinary American criminal courts. The reference to socialist (meaning: state Communist) comrades' courts is hardly reassuring. They were coercive arms of authoritarian states. And whatever else they accomplished in the way of dispute resolution, their highest priority was always state security.[9] These courts have by now been normalized, as

---

[7] Richard Danzig, "Towards a Complementary, Decentralized System of Criminal Justice," in *Neighborhood Justice: An Emerging Idea*, ed. Roman Tomasic & Malcolm Feeley (New York: Longman, 1982), 17. These "retreats" are for corporate executives, company-organized. They are for morale-building, not dispute resolution. A classic send-up of these bizarre rituals is in the first novel by Kurt Vonnegut, Jr., *Player Piano* (New York: Delacorte Press, 1952). When he wrote the book, Vonnegut was a public relations officer for General Electric. He resigned before it was published. Richard Danzig can't tell the difference between a tribal moot and the Bohemian Grove. He has never attended a tribal moot, but he is elite enough that he may have attended the Bohemian Grove.

[8] William L.F. Felstiner & Lynne A. Williams, "Mediation as an Alternative to Criminal Prosecution," *Law & Human Behavior* 2(3) (1980), 233.

[9] Harold J. Berman & James W. Spindler, "Soviet Comrades' Courts," *U. of Chicago*

the Russian, Chinese and Cuban regimes have reconciled with capitalism.

Originally, the establishment wanted alternatives to adjudication—for other people. It wanted to limit access to the courts. The "litigation explosion" quickly became a cliché. The courts were supposedly swamped, mostly by the little people with their little problems. Surely alternate dispute resolution (ADR) was the answer. And the core ADR nostrum was mediation.

A social science theory got into the picture. In the late 1960s, there was a famous study, by the Vera Institute of Justice, of the processing of felony cases in New York City. The politicians and the newspaper editors were concerned about what they called the "deterioration" of these cases.[10] This just means that very few cases went to trial. Look at what's happening! First the problem was supposed to be too many cases. Now the problem was not enough cases. Somehow, it was concluded that these problems had the same solution.

The study made the genuinely startling discovery that most felony arrests involved people in some sort of prior relationship. Felonies are the serious crimes in Anglo-American law, such as manslaughter, which is what Mr. A was convicted of. For rape, 83% of arrests involved prior relationships. For homicide, it was 50%. Felonious assault: 69%. Even some property crimes fit the picture: 36% of robberies and 39% of burglaries. *These* are the cases that deteriorate. Often the complainant and the defendant reconciled because of their relationship. Or

---

L. Rev. 45 (1978): 842–910; Jesse Berman, "The Cuban Popular Tribunals," *Columbia L. Rev.* 69(8) (Dec. 1969): 1317–1354; Sally Engle Merry, "Defining 'Success' in the Neighborhood Justice Movement," in *Neighborhood Justice*, 174.

10 A study of homicides in Houston, covering about the same time period, found that these cases deteriorated at all stages, beginning even before they *were* cases: police made many fewer arrests. In a category of cases in most of which the grand jury returned a "no bill," *i.e.,* refused to indict, terminating the prosecution, that was the determination in 40.26% where victim and killer were relatives, in 36.77% where they were friends or associates, and in only 23.64% of cases where they were strangers to each other. This indicates that it is not merely because of decisions by prosecutors and judges—by system professionals—that cases deteriorate. Henry P. Lundsgaarde, "Murder in Space City," in *The Social Organization of Law*, 133–156. Grand juries are ad hoc panels of lay persons.

witnesses didn't show up for preliminary hearings. Or a complainant might get somebody arrested, not to get him prosecuted, but just to harass him for his bad behavior.

These continuing relationships weren't usually multiplex relationships, but they resemble them in one very important way. To the disputants, their continuing relationship is often more important than their current dispute, so they do not resort to litigation. For the same reason, disputes between businesses are often not litigated.[11] Some academics therefore proposed that mediation was the best way to deal with prior relationships cases. After all, in the anthropological literature, offenses usually involved people in relationships, or who knew each other. So, let us mediate prior relationship cases too. So said the U.S. Department of Justice, along with conservative judges, several of the more intellectual members of the legal elite and some quasi-scholars at think tanks. All the new mediation agencies focused on prior relationship cases.

B. *Neighborhood Justice Centers*

In the early 1970s, the call for alternate dispute resolution went out from no less than Warren Burger, Chief Justice of the U.S. Supreme Court. Americans, he declaimed, were too litigious, and so there was too much litigation. They were wasting the precious time of judges (but that's what we pay them for!). The most powerful judge and lawyer in the United States—in the world!—repeatedly denounced judges and lawyers: but "[t]he concerns were not with justice, but with harmonious relations, with community, with removing 'garbage cases' from the courts. Nonjudicial means were suggested as a means of dispute handling."[12]

---

[11] Stewart Macauley, "Non-Contractual Relations in Business: A Preliminary Study," *American Sociological Rev.* 28(1) (Feb. 1963): 55–67.

[12] Laura Nader, "When Is Popular Justice Popular?" in *The Possibility of Popular Justice: A Case Study of Community Mediation in the United States*, ed. Sally Engle Merry & Neal Milner (Ann Arbor, MI: University of Michigan Press, 1993), 441. Nader, an anthropologist—the sister of lawyer-activist Ralph Nader—believes that Burger was prompted by his chief aide Mark Cannon, "a man of Mormon background, whose philosophy reflects the Mormon idea of community and consensus and the

This was a neat trick. The rhetoric of the left—peace, love, community and harmony—was turned against it. And that worked, at least to the extent that, although there was no popular demand or support for ADR, neither was there any popular opposition to it. United in support of the federal Dispute Resolution Act were, among others, "the National Chambers of Commerce and Ralph Nader's consumer advocates; the Conference of Chief Justices and 1960s-style community activist groups; and the American Bar Association and vociferous critics of professionalism."[13]

The U.S. Department of Justice financed three pilot programs in the late 1970s. These agencies, which I have already mentioned, were called Neighborhood Justice Centers, or NJCs. This was not in response to any grass-roots popular movement for court reform. It was originated by the national government in response to proposals by legal and judicial elites.[14] There was no concern for rights or due process, only for smoothing over conflict.[15]

The claims on behalf of the as yet nonexistent NJCs were extravagant. They were supposed to do all sorts of great things. Among other things, they were supposed to:

(1) save time and money;
(2) reduce court caseloads;
(3) foster "community" in local neighborhoods;
(4) provide "satisfaction" to involved parties;
(5) make people feel better about the justice system.

They did none of these things.

1. They didn't save any time or money. They didn't save time, because mediation involved lots of meetings, and it took

---

Mormon dislike of courts and lawyers [citations omitted]." *Id.*; *cf.* Mark Cannon, "Contentious and Burdensome Litigation," *Phi Kappa Phi Journal* (1986): 10–12. Fringe religious types also pioneered a later form of ADL, "Restorative Justice" (*infra*).

13 Daniel McGillis, "Minor Dispute Processing: A Review of Recent Developments," in *Neighborhood Justice*, 63.

14 Roman Tomasic & Malcolm M. Feeley, "Introduction," *Neighborhood Justice*, xi; Nader, "When Is Popular Justice Popular?" 441–42, 447.

15 *E.g.*, Sander, "Varieties of Dispute Processing," 37.

longer than court processing, whereas most court cases deteriorate anyway before much time passes. They didn't save money either. Where there's any evidence, as for Dorchester, Massachusetts, mediation was two or three times as expensive as adjudication.[16] A later, multi-year, multi-million-dollar study concluded that there were no cost savings or time savings when mediation, early neutral evaluation and other devices were used after legal proceedings commenced.[17] As late as 2005, there was no evidence that mediation was cost-effective.[18]

2. They didn't reduce judicial caseloads very much. Only a small number of cases went to mediation. And many of them came back to court when mediation failed. The vast majority of cases, civil and criminal, are resolved without trial *or* mediation. Anyway, if courts are such a great idea, why is it so important to keep some people out of them? If mediation is such a great idea, why not mediate almost everything, as is done in many primitive societies?

3. Mediation didn't promote community. Neighborhood Justice Centers didn't grow out of communities. They were inserted into them. Mediators were mostly strangers from outside the community, of higher social status and often of a different race (*i.e.,* they were mostly white, unlike most of the disputants).[19] Richard Danzig assumed a degree of social solidarity which just doesn't exist in impoverished urban slums, or even in many other areas, such as suburbia.

In the Tonga, Ifugao and Kpelle examples, disputants

---

16 William L.F. Felsteiner & Lynne Williams, *Community Mediation in Dorchester, Massachusetts* (Washington DC: U.S. Department of Justice, 1980), 42.

17 J. Kakalik *et al.*, *An Evaluation of Early Mediation and Neutral Evaluation Under the Civil Justice Reform Act* (Santa Monica, CA: RAND Institute of Justice, 1996); Menkel-Meadow, "Roots and Inspirations," 25. Thus the RAND Corporation's own research discredited their former employee Richard Danzig's absurd, but absurdly influential reveries about complementary, decentralized justice.

18 Moffitt & Bordone, "Perspectives on Dispute Resolution," 25.

19 Felsteiner & Williams, "Community Mediation," 150; Merry, "Sorting Out Popular Justice," 59; Yngvesson, "Local People, Local Problems," 395.

came from villages occupied by several hundred, mostly interrelated people. Everybody knew everybody else, in person or by reputation. You rarely find that now in urban or suburban areas of the United States where most Americans live: "In contemporary mediation centers in the United States, few if any of these features of mediation [as practiced in "small-scale societies"] will be found."[20] To approximate mediation in primitive societies, NJCs "must serve very small populations rather than districts containing several thousand residents who do not know one another nor expect to deal with one another in the future."[21] In Kansas City, the NJC was not located in a neighborhood with a sense of solidarity and neighborliness. The "target population" (a revealing phrase) was the inhabitants of a police patrol area, approximately 53,000 people.[22]

The NJCs served so-called "neighborhoods" of tens of thousands of people. Most of their residents knew very few of the other residents. And most of the mediators weren't from the neighborhoods they worked in.[23] A Kansas City prosecutor identified the targets: "poor white trash," not the deserving poor.[24] The parties didn't choose the mediator. That isn't, strictly speaking, a requirement for mediation, but it's usually how it's done in primitive societies where mediation is more successful. Nor did the disputants have to approve the mediator, who was simply assigned to their case. (Actually, it was usually

---

20 Roman Tomasic, "Mediation as an Alternative to Adjudication," 231; Merry, "Defining 'Success,'" 176–77.

21 Sally E. Merry, "A Plea for Thinking How Dispute Resolution Works," *The Mooter* 2(4) (1979), 39.

22 Christine B. Harrington, *Shadow Justice: The Ideology and Institutionalization of Alternatives to Court* (Westport, CT & London: Greenwood Press, 1985), 109–110.

23 In Cambridge, Massachusetts, an investigator found a "pattern of relatively young, highly educated, predominantly white mediators serving a predominantly poor, racially mixed population of litigants." This was also true of San Francisco. Sally Engle Merry, "Sorting Out Popular Justice," *The Possibility of Popular Justice*, 59. Another description: the volunteers were "predominantly female, predominantly white, relatively young, well-educated, aspiring professionals . . . " Yngvesson, "Local People, Local Problems," 395. They were yuppies. Today they would be called hipsters.

24 Harrington, *Shadow Justice*, 149.

several mediators.) That *is* a requirement for mediation.

In a large, complex, socially differentiated society, where would mediation work best? It would work best in stable, homogenous communities of civic-minded people. In other words, in the United States, rich white neighborhoods or suburbs. A gated community would be ideal. In Boston, they put the NJC in Dorchester, where people are working class or poor or both. They should have put it in, for example, Brookline, which is a wealthy Jewish suburb: a much more homogeneous community than Dorchester. But for several reasons, they didn't.

One reason is that the unstated purpose of the scheme was to pacify the poor. The affluent don't need to be pacified. People in Brookline are satisfied with the regular court system. The law functions to serve the interests of their kind of people. They are mostly homeowners, businessmen, landlords and professionals. In Brookline, mediation would be a solution without a problem. In Dorchester, there's a problem, but mediation is not the solution.

This isn't just speculation on my part. An NJC was set up in Suffolk County, New York City suburbs which, like Brookline, are affluent, white, and mostly Jewish. 40% of the cases were not resolved, usually because the defendant wouldn't participate. But that was a higher success rate than in the other NJCs.[25]

I'll postpone Point Four, about how satisfying the experience was, for a little later.

You will recall that Danzig wanted a "complementary" system. What usually happened was that the courts used mediation to try to reduce their caseloads. (Caseloads don't have to be high for judges and prosecutors to wish they were even lower in order to reduce their workload.) Prosecutors had to agree to each referral. Prosecutors often agreed to reduce *their* caseloads by allowing what they called "garbage cases" to go to mediation. These were cases where they were not sure they

---
25 Merry, "Defining 'Success,'" 176.

would win or cases they thought weren't worth their trouble. Most of these cases would never have gone to trial.[26]

As one prosecutor explained:

> Neighborhood justice is really handy because it is like a garbage dump: they will take and deal with cases which we simply are not set up to handle. I just like them because they are handy. I wish I could get rid of more garbage that way.[27]

So mediation was a way to widen the field of social control, which is contrary to what some of its proponents expected.[28] Some NJC advocates fancied that mediation would somehow facilitate de-legalization. But systems of informal justice generally widen the net of social control.[29]

Usually these programs made some provision for people to bring in their own disputes for mediation, bypassing the court. But people didn't do that. In Dorchester, there were eight walk-ins in two years. In court-ordered, prosecutor-approved mediation, mediators told the parties that if mediation failed, the case would go back to court, and the judge would be unhappy. The judge sent them to mediation because he never wanted to see them again. If they came back, the defendant would be viewed as uncooperative and unreasonable. The mediators were threatening the defendant.[30] This is not a voluntary process.

NJCs were new, so few people had heard of them. The NJC in Los Angeles had an aggressive outreach program, a publicity campaign. Over 50% of the cases were walk-ins. Another

---

[26] Harrington, *Shadow Justice*, 122–23

[27] Quoted in Harrington, *Shadow Justice*, 147.

[28] Harrington, *Shadow Justice*, 170–71.

[29] Richard L. Abel, "The Contradictions of Informal Justice," in *The Politics of Informal Justice*, ed. Richard L. Abel (New York: Academic Press, 1980), 1: 267–301. "Informalism expands the capacity of the justice system to manage minor conflicts and legitimates the extension of state intervention on functionalist grounds." Harrington, *Shadow Justice*, 170. This is why the Philippine dictator Marcos instituted the Barangay courts.

[30] Harrington, *Shadow Justice*, 122–23; Merry, "Defining 'Success,'" 178–79.

one-third were referrals by courts or the police. The mediators handled 50 cases a month, which is a very small number, in a city of millions. I count it as a success if the parties reach a mediated agreement and comply with it. I consider it a failure if the case doesn't lead to a mediated agreement, or if that agreement isn't followed. Measured in this way, there were maybe 1,150 successes and 2,850 failures.[31]

I say "maybe" because the statistics are presented in misleading ways. The investigators were advocates for NJCs, but even they report that the court-referred cases had an 82% success rate, whereas the genuinely voluntary cases had a 14–36% success rate. Government coercion makes a big difference.

What if an NJC accepted *only* walk-ins? I know of only one program like that: the San Francisco Community Boards. It was also unusual in that several of these Boards served somewhat smaller neighborhoods than is usual. That's where mediation works best, in theory. But their populations ranged from 17,117 to 105,592.[32] I lived in the biggest neighborhood, Bernal Heights, for two years. I never heard of its Community Board, although I had some neighbor conflicts, including one tenant/landlord lawsuit. All the San Francisco Boards together processed only 365 cases a year, in a city of 640,000 people.[33] The cost per referral was $750, as compared with $350 in Dorchester.[34]

There were few cases, but many mediators: at any one time, 350 to 400 enthusiastic volunteers—more mediators than cases! *They* got a lot of satisfaction out of mediation, which often served as "a vehicle for personal growth"—for themselves.[35] That's very California. Only 11% of their cases came

---

31 Janice A. Roehl & Royer F. Cook, "The Neighborhood Justice Centers Field Test," in *Neighborhood Justice*, 91–110.

32 Frederic L. DuBow & Craig McEwen, "Community Boards: An Analytic Profile," *The Possibility of Popular Justice*, 130.

33 Ibid., 127.

34 Ibid., 148.

35 Barbara Yngvesson, "Local People, Local Problems, and Neighborhood Justice: The Discourse of 'Community' in San Francisco Community Boards," *The Possibility*

from court referrals, possibly reducing court caseloads by a few cases. But mediation was supposed to reduce caseloads substantially. In reality, it had almost no effect. It never does. In Atlanta, for instance, the NJC received most of its cases from the courts (nearly 50% were referred by court clerks, and almost 25% by judges), but it processed, at most, 2% as many cases as the lower trial courts.[36]

Community Boards are also exceptional in another, ironic way. They rarely deal with prior-relationship cases.[37] That's probably why they are, in a relatively small way, successful.

The fundamental reason why studies claiming success for mediation can't be substantiated is that there are no control groups. We know that judges and prosecutors don't randomly assign some cases to adjudication and others to mediation. The "garbage cases" go to mediation. We'd like to know what would happen if all cases remained in court. Everywhere, most cases are dismissed before trial. One of my Berkeley professors studied two lower trial courts in Connecticut. Those are the courts with jurisdiction over misdemeanors, which are the less serious crimes. In a two-month period, *no* cases went to trial.[38] Trials are rare, and increasingly so, in state and federal courts.[39]

The original three NJCs were financed by the U.S. Department of Justice. Malcolm M. Feeley writes: "A proposal to treat these experimental programs as true experiments and randomly assign would-be clients or leave them to their own devices was explicitly and firmly rejected by the Department of Justice."[40] I have read only one study of a court which did

---

of Popular Justice, 295.

36 Roehl & Cook, "The Neighborhood Justice Centers Field Test," 95, 96.

37 Royer F. Cook, Janice A. Roehl, & David I. Sheppard, *Neighborhood Justice Centers Field Test—Final Evaluation Report* (Washington, DC: American Bar Association, 1980), 6.

38 Feeley, *The Process Is the Punishment*, 251.

39 Marc Galanter, "The Vanishing Trial: An Examination of Trials and Related Matters in Federal and State Courts," *J. of Empirical and Legal Studies* (1) (2004): 459– 570.

40 Feeley, *Court Reform on Trial*, 112.

randomly assign some of the cases to the NJC. That was in Brooklyn, New York—the study was privately funded by the Vera Institute of Justice (the "continuing relationships" people)—and it dealt with felony cases, as had the Institute's influential study of arrest "deterioration," *Felony Arrests*.

In the control group, 70% of cases were either dismissed or were adjourned in contemplation of dismissal. In the latter situation, the case is postponed for six months, and if the defendant hasn't gotten arrested again, the case is dismissed.[41][42] 3% of defendants were sentenced to jail terms, which means one year or less, although they were arrested for felonies, which are punishable by imprisonment for more than a year. Their charges were reduced. Only 1% were referred to the grand jury, which decides whether there should be a felony prosecution. Since the grand jury does not always indict (although it usually does), that means that less than 1% of felony arrests led to felony trials. Fewer still led to convictions, although I assume that most trials resulted in convictions.

4. I return to Point Four (satisfaction). In the NJC group, only 56% of the cases were mediated. In the other cases, the victim or the defendant (or both) didn't show up. Where mediation led to an agreement, the participants reported higher satisfaction with the system than for the court group, but the difference was not great. These reports of high satisfaction are, however, worthless since they are based only on clients who completed the mediation process. They ignore disputants who decided at some point not to participate.[43] In Brooklyn, where there was random assignment and a control group, mediation made some people feel better. But "there was little evidence that mediation was more effective than court adjudication in preventing recidivism during the four-month follow-up period."[44]

---

[41] Davis, "Mediation: The Brooklyn Experiment," 170 n. 5.

[42] I once went through this! I was not rearrested. The system works.

[43] Harrington, *Shadow Justice*, 142–43.

[44] Davis, "Mediation: The Brooklyn Experiment," 163.

5. I have no objection to a process that makes people "feel better," unless they are being played. But there was little evidence that mediation had fully or finally resolved the problems between the parties. This was measured by how often new problems were reported by the plaintiff, by the frequency of their calling the police again and by arrests of either party for a crime committed against the other party. On these metrics there was no significant difference between the mediation group and the court group.[45] Although there are studies of how participants felt, I know of only one study of whether they perceived the process as just or fair. In Brooklyn, 88% thought that their mediation was fair, compared to 76% who thought their adjudication was fair. That's not a big difference. And even that is after more than 70% of the cases had been dismissed.[46] Complainants are never asked if they feel the dismissal of their cases was fair. The answer is obvious.

The final irony of the NJC debacle is this. Mediation was supposed to be especially effective in prior-relationship cases. That was their main selling point. But mediation is *least* effective in property disputes and in disputes arising from long-standing relationships.[47]

C. *The Prior History of Informal Justice in America*

The NJC movement—if an elite-initiated, state-controlled phenomenon can be called a "movement"—was not the first of its kind. It sought alternatives to the regular court system.

---

45 Harrington, *Shadow Justice*, 143–44. Proponents of mediation have quietly dropped this claim: "The language of resolution implies a level of finality that is only occasionally a realistic condition." Moffitt & Bordone, "Perspectives on Dispute Resolution," 4. This is true of mediation generally, not just in NJCs. Gulliver, "On Mediators," 20 n. 8.

46 Robert C. Davis, Martha Tichane, & Deborah Grayson, *Mediation and Arbitration as Alternatives to Prosecution in Felony Arrest Cases—An Evaluation of the Brooklyn Dispute Resolution Center* (New York: Vera Institute of Justice, 1979), 50, 52.

47 Dispute Resolution Alternatives Committee, *The Citizen Dispute Settlement Process in Florida—A Study of Five Programs* (n.p.; Office of the State Court Administrator, Florida Supreme Court, 1979), 55; Felsteiner & Williams, "Mediation as an Alternative to Criminal Prosecution," 66–68; Tomasic, "Mediation as an Alternative to Adjudication," 236.

It sought procedural informality. It sought to individualize justice. It sought non-punitive dispositions which were conciliatory, rehabilitative, or even therapeutic. It sought to get to the social "roots" of interpersonal conflicts. These goals and methods were also among the goals and methods of the Progressive-era juvenile-court movement, which was supposed to humanize the official treatment of children who were causing trouble and committing crimes. In the framework of the juvenile court movement, troubled or troublesome children received a new social identity: they were "juvenile delinquents."[48] Reformists claimed that these youths would be helped, and healed, by a fatherly juvenile court judge, by social workers, and by "diversion" out of the regular criminal justice system and prisons into custodial facilities tailored to their needs.

Although the juvenile justice system, like the NJC system, is now almost universally regarded as a total failure,[49] there are now proposals to *combine* these failures! Mediation for juvenile delinquents![50] Failure squared![51]

Yet, the informal justice reformers soldiered on. Their next reform was small-claims courts. The Small Claims Court movement has taken as its premise that small cases are simple cases and that therefore a pared-down judicial procedure is what is called for. Next to the juvenile court, there has probably been no legal institution that was more ballyhooed as a great legal innovation. Despite this ballyhoo, the evidence now seems overwhelming that that the Small Claims Court

---

[48] Anthony M. Platt, *The Child Savers: The Invention of Delinquency* (2nd, enl. ed.; Chicago, IL: University of Chicago Press, 1977); Robert M. Mannel, *Thorns & Thistles: Juvenile Delinquents in the United States, 1825–1940* (Hanover, NH: University Press of New England, 1973).

[49] *A New Juvenile Justice System: Total Reform of a Broken System*, ed. Nancy E. Dowd (New York & London: New York University Press, 2015).

[50] *Restorative Justice for Juveniles: Conferencing, Mediation and Circles*, ed. Allison Morris & Gabrielle Maxwell (Oxford, England & Portland, OR: Hart Publishing, 2001).

[51] Actually, that would be something like Richard Danzig's absurd example, the loitering juvenile.

has failed its original purpose; that the individuals for whom it was designed have turned out to be its victims.[52]

One of the assumptions there was that "small" cases are simple cases which do not require much judicial time or expertise. Simple people, simple problems. This assumption is often false.[53] A seemingly simple case such as a landlord's lawsuit to evict a tenant for nonpayment of rent may implicate a complex body of law—if the law were taken seriously. Small claims courts often have jurisdiction over these summary eviction cases. But "the evidence now seems overwhelming that the Small Claims Court has failed its original purpose; that the individuals for whom it was designed have become its victims."[54]

In practice, small claims courts function as an eviction service for slumlords and a collection agency for ghetto businesses. Nonetheless, such courts have been institutionalized everywhere. Once that happens, it no longer matters whether the court serves its original purpose, or any purpose. It always serves power and the servants of power. And it is always self-serving.

A decade before the NJC movement, another court reform scheme, pre-trial diversion, had some of the same goals as the NJC, with similar rhetoric and rationale. But diversion programs rarely succeeded.[55] They were optional for courts, and prosecutors had to consent to diversion, just as they did in NJC mediation. As later with the NJCs, "many prosecutors came to regard diversion as an alternative penalty for marginal offenders."[56] What Malcolm Feeley wrote in 1982 proved to

---

52 Sander, "Varieties of Dispute Processing," 33. This article is considered to be "the 'Big Bang' of modern dispute resolution and practice." Moffitt & Bordone, "Perspectives on Dispute Resolution," 19. If it all began with a bang it has ended, in the words of T.S. Eliot, in a whimper. But in an institutionalized, well-funded whimper, which will echo on.

53 Barbara B. Yngvesson & P. Hennessey, "Small Claims, Complex Disputes: A Review of the Small Claims Literature," *Law & Soc'y Rev.* 9 (1975): 219– 274.

54 Sander, "Varieties of Dispute Processing," 33.

55 Feeley, *Court Reform on Trial*, 108.

56 Feeley, *Court Reform on Trial*, 105; Sally Baker & Susan Sadd, *Court Employment Project Evaluation Final Report* (New York: Vera Institute of Justice, 1979).

be prophetic: "What pretrial diversion was to court reform in the1970s, neighborhood justice or dispute settlement centers are becoming in the 1980s. They are the new cure-all."[57] Generally, he observes, "criminal justice policy is often characterized by a preoccupation with short-term outcomes and—all too often—with gimmickry."[58]

As far as I can tell, the NJC movement as such is extinct. Its "possible demise"—and the reasons for it—was anticipated as early as 1982.[59] Something similar is now going on, here and there, under other names, such as "community mediation centers." But in the 2005 *Handbook of Dispute Resolution* (a 546 page "handbook"), there is only one sentence on neighborhood dispute resolution—in the article on "Roots and Inspirations."[60] NJCs are history.

I've come across self-congratulatory accounts of two mediation centers which, as of 2013, were still in business.[61] One (the only one) in Philadelphia, is operated by Roman Catholic nuns, and is described as a "neighborhood justice center." The other (also the only one there) is in the Borough of Queens, New York City. Despite having "community" in their names, these centers each service a catchment area of over three million people. Both get most of their cases from court referrals or other government referrals. The center in Queens annually

---

57 Feeley, *Court Reform on Trial*, 109. These programs never learn the lessons of their predecessors: "Crisis thinking lacks historical perspective." Ibid., 192.

58 Brian Williams, *Victims of Crime and Community Justice* (London & Philadelphia, PA: Jessica Kingsley Publishers, 2005), 127 (note the unintentional ambiguity of the title).

59 Merry, "Defining 'Success,'" 172.

60 Menkel-Meadow, "Roots and Inspirations," 19–20.

61 Cheryl Catrona, "Fitting the Fuss to the Community Mediation Center Forum," *Dispute Resolution Mag.* (Winter 2013): 11–15 (Philadelphia); Mark Kleiman, "Mending the Fabric of Community," *Dispute Resolution Mag.* (Winter 2013): 16 (Queens). Pope John Paul II spoke of "mending the Christian fabric of society." Quoted in Petros Willey, "Editor's Note: Mending the Fabric," *The Sower* 33(4), available at https://catechetics.com/editors-note-mending-the-fabric. Not all societies are woven out of Christian fabrics. Charles Colson, the Watergate felon turned Evangelical, joined the RJ movement (he operated Christian private prisons). Wayne Northey, review of *Justice That Restored*, by Charles Colson (2018), www.academia.edu.

receives 1,500 cases from courts and 500 walk-ins, which is the highest proportion of walk-ins I know of anywhere, but 75% are still involuntary referrals.

Undoubtedly some people walk in to preempt prosecution or litigation. Keeping even 2,000 cases out of the courts in Queens would have a very small impact on court caseloads, even if we didn't know what the author doesn't tell us: that many cases would not have gone to trial, and many mediated cases would return to court later. In Philadelphia, only 30% of referrals were mediated at all, and surely these were not all success stories. But the author of the article on the Philadelphia center is right about one thing: "Conflict resolution is a growth industry."[62]

Now there is a new cure-all: "Restorative Justice" (RJ). Not to keep you in suspense, I will later conclude that, what pretrial diversion was to court reform in the 1970s, and what neighborhood justice centers were to court reform in the 1980s, Restorative Justice is since the 1990s.

If a new quack panacea has come along even more recently, I haven't heard of it yet.

---

62 Cutrona, "Fitting the Fuss," 11.

6. Conclusion for Reformists

I CONCLUDE THAT IN THE SHORT TERM, court-ordered mediation isn't much better, and maybe isn't *any* better, than adjudication is in prior relationship cases. It seems still more clear that, over a longer period, it isn't better at all. Mediation is probably keeping some cases from going to court where the defendant might do better in adjudication. In courts, you have some rights (although the rights of victims as such are nonexistent or minimal, and rarely exercised[1]). In mediation, you have no rights, and no lawyer. But you get a great big hug. And so does the mediator.

The most common way to resolve chronic conflict in a relationship in an urban society is to *end* the relationship, despite the costs and hardships which may ensue.[2] Curiously, that's also the most common solution in the band societies of hunter-gatherers. Foragers don't remain for long in one place anyway. Individuals move away. Or, the group splits and part of it moves away. But this isn't always easy to do in a modern urban society, where people are burdened with jobs, leases, dependents, mortgages, etc.

I promised to provide two lessons. My lesson to legal

---

[1] Robert C. Black, "Forgotten Penological Purposes: A Critique of Victim Participation in Sentencing," *American J. of Jurisprudence* (1994): 225–240, available online at http://scholarship.lawnd.edu/ajj/vol39/issI/9.

[2] And as Lon L. Fuller wrote, "mediation can be directed, not toward cementing a relationship, but toward terminating it." "Mediation—Its Forms and Functions," 129. So can adjudication—divorce, for instance.

reformers is: *disputing processes which work in primitive societies usually won't work in modern societies.* "It may be difficult or impossible to transplant a mode of conflict management between socially different settings."[3] The form—mediation for instance—looks about the same. But the social content and the social context are completely different. This is equally true of the next reform to come along, Restorative Justice.

There are drastic differences between primitive and modern societies. In primitive societies, individuals are imbedded in groups. Conflicts between individuals almost always directly implicate the groups they belong to.[4] There are usually some people with their own interests at stake who actively involve themselves in resolving the problem. The dispute is really between groups, and so is the mediation. In the NJCs, every dispute was treated as a conflict between two individuals. The Centers usually refused to bring in third parties. Probably that wasn't feasible.[5] But that is only to say that NJC mediation wasn't feasible.

Another drastic difference between primitive and modern societies is that all primitive anarchist societies are more egalitarian than all modern state societies. The very existence of the state establishes a huge inequality. The criminal law (which is specific to the state) treats certain disputes as between the state and an individual accused of crime. No matter how many rights you give the defendant, the state always has more power. And for many years, American courts have been reducing the rights of those suspected or accused of crime.[6] The state decides whether to respect those rights, and the police, the prosecutor and the judge are all part of the state. I mentioned that the prosecutor had a veto on sending cases to mediation.

---

3 Black, "Elementary Forms of Conflict Management," 94 n. 32.

4 Roberts, *Order and Dispute*, 49.

5 Fuller, "Mediation," 133.

6 Leonard W. Levy, *Against the Law: The Supreme Court and Criminal Justice* (New York: Harper & Row, 1974); Yale Kamisar, "The 'Police Practices' Phases of the Criminal Process and Three Phases of the Burger Court," in *The Burger Years: Right and Wrong in the Burger Court, 1969–1986*, ed. Herman Schwartz (New York: Viking, Elisabeth Sifton Books, 1987), 143–168.

The prosecutor never participates in mediation.

These state societies are also class societies. The state always upholds social hierarchy. The state *is* a social hierarchy. But some of the most important personal and interpersonal problems are rooted in the economy and the social structure. The parties are often unequal in wealth and power. Tenants and landlords, husbands and wives, businesses and consumers, bosses and workers—they're usually not equal. Pretending that they're equal doesn't equalize them. People who are unequal before they enter the legal system will still be unequal when they leave it.[7] But maybe the weaker party got a warm fuzzy feeling from the nice mediator (or mediatrix) listening to her problems. She might feel better for awhile. It doesn't mean that she received justice. At best, for awhile, she may just think she did. But there is no evidence even of that.

Justice is not, for me, the highest social value. Mine is freedom. I am all for justice, but the conditions required for freedom take priority. No kind of Alternate Dispute Resolution even purports to enhance freedom. And I doubt that ADR delivers justice any more than does traditional adjudication, which itself is far from living up to the promise of—these words are inscribed on the U.S. Supreme Court building—equal justice under law.

---

[7] Merry, "Defining 'Success' in the Neighborhood Justice Movement," 182.

7. The Incomplete Anarchist Critique of Criminal Law

ANARCHISTS HAVE A LOT of excuses for their unpopularity. They've suffered military and police repression. In the newspapers, as in the history books, they're either lied about or ignored. They get very resentful about the stereotype of the bomb-throwing anarchist. Some people are rude to them. Others mock them. Most ignore them. It's so unfair. Bomb-throwing? We stopped doing that weeks ago! (Except in Athens. I've seen videos.)

But even if anarchists don't throw bombs, some people do. Even fair-minded people reasonably ask: if there's no state, who will protect us from aggressors and predators?[1] The article I first discussed, about the Plateau Tonga, was written by Elizabeth Colson for the express purpose of answering that question.

The traditional anarchist answer is obviously inadequate. The anarchists say that by abolishing private property, we eliminate almost all reasons for people to quarrel. My examples—the Plateau Tonga, the Ifugao and the Kpelle—refute that argument. The vast majority of cases in the Kpelle moot, for instance, involved conjugal disputes and rights over women (not the rights *of* women, rights *over* women).[2] There

---

[1] Donald F. Busky, *Communism in History and Theory: From Utopian Socialism to the Fall of the Soviet Union* (Westport, CT & London: Praeger, 2002), 105.

[2] James L. Gibbs, Jr., "Law and Personality: Suggestions for a New Direction," in *Law*

are primitive anarchist societies, the hunter-gatherers, which have even less property than the Kpelle. The Bushmen, for instance, were until recently, to put it bluntly, communists.[3] They rarely quarreled over property, because they hardly had any. But they did quarrel. Their homicide rate in the 1960s was even higher than the high American homicide rate in the 1960s.[4] Peter Kropotkin, in the 1890s, praised the Bushmen as friendly, benevolent and generous: they "used to hunt in common, and divided the spoil without quarreling; . . ."[5] Food sharing is in fact an aspect of the "generalized reciprocity" which is a universal feature of hunter-gatherer society.[6] The Bushmen worked cooperatively and shared food communally. But Kropotkin was mistaken to assume that, consequently, they never quarreled. Work and food are not the only things people quarrel about. The main source of quarrels among the Bushmen, as among the Kpelle, was jealousy.

Kropotkin characterized the Papuans, also, as "primitive communists."[7] They are of course also anarchists. But in at least one Papuan society, a dispute over a pig could escalate into a war.[8] Communism + anarchy ≠ perpetual peace.

Among societies such as the Plateau Tonga and the Ifugaos, the possibility of feud—interminable mutual retaliation—was recognized, and feared, but not always avoided. Some primitive societies made little effort to avoid it. However, Kropotkin, along with Engels, was correct to say that the spectre of eternal

---

in Culture and Society, 188 (Table 1).

3 Richard B. Lee, "Reflections on Primitive Communism," in *Hunters and Gatherers*, ed. Tim Ingold, David Riches, & James Woodburn (London: Berg Publishers, 1990), 1: 252–268; idem, "Primitive Communism and the Origin of Social Equality," in *The Evolution of Political Systems: Socio-Politics in Small-Scale Sedentary Societies*, ed. Steadman Upham (Cambridge: Cambridge University Press, 1990), 225–246.

4 Lee, *The !Kung San*, ch. 13.

5 Kropotkin, *Mutual Aid*, 89.

6 Lee, *The !Kung San*, 437.

7 Kropotkin, *Mutual Aid*, 95.

8 Koch, *War and Peace in Jalémó*.

feud has been exaggerated. Eventually feuds are composed,[9] or else they simply wane. But Kropotkin was wrong to blame feuds on "superstition," specifically, witchcraft.[10] This is a quaint 19th century freethinker prejudice. Witchcraft furnished a supposed means, not a motive, for inflicting harm. Blaming witchcraft for feuds is like blaming spears for feuds. Among the Iroquois, the kinfolk of a murder or witchcraft victim were expected usually to accept compensation.[11]

"We already foresee a state of society," wrote Peter Kropotkin in 1887, "where the liberty of the individual will be limited by no laws, no bonds—by nothing else but his own social habits and the necessity, which everyone feels, of finding cooperation, support, and sympathy among his neighbors."[12] But social habits and felt necessities have not eliminated disputes from anarchist primitive societies.[13] Bakunin expressed, in all its innocent purity, the anarchist party line: "The organization of society being always and everywhere the sole cause of the crimes committed by men, it is evidently hypocritical or nonsensical for society to punish criminals, every punishment being based upon a presumption of culpability and criminals being at no time culpable."[14] At no time culpable?

---

9 Kropotkin, *Mutual Aid*, 108–109; John Bossy, "Postscript," *Disputes and Settlements*, 288 n. 1; Frederick Engels, "Origin of the Family, Private Property and the State," Karl Marx & Frederick Engels, *Selected Works in One Volume* (Moscow, USSR: Progress Publishers & New York: International Publishers, 1968), 520, 528. Engels' source is Lewis Henry Morgan, *League of the Iroquois* (Secaucus, NJ: Citadel Press, 1969), 330–33.

10 Kropotkin, *Mutual Aid*, 94–95. The feud (more like a war) recounted by Koch had nothing to do with "superstition." It was provoked by the theft (or recovery) of a pig, not by witchcraft accusations. Koch, "Pigs and Politics in the New Guinea Highlands."

11 Anthony F.C. Wallace, *The Death and Rebirth of the Seneca* (New York: Vintage Books, 1969), 25–26, 30.

12 "Anarchist Communism: Its Basis and Principles," in *Kropotkin's Revolutionary Pamphlets*, ed. Roger N. Baldwin (New York: Dover Publications, 1970), 63.

13 "I have never heard of any society that was free of problems nor any society in which members did not have to engage in discussion to work out ways of action." Herbert Blumer, "The Methodological Position of Symbolic Interactionism," *Symbolic Interactionism: Perspective and Method* (Englewood Cliffs, NJ: Prentice-Hall, 1969), 18.

14 "Program and Object of the Secret Revolution of the International Brethren

Most people would agree with historian Hippolyte Taine, writing in 1877: "However bad a particular government may be, there is something still worse, and that is the suppression of all government."[15] Most people have never heard arguments for a reasonable alternative. Someone with reasonable concerns about her personal safety, and the protection of what little property he owns, will not be reassured by airy nothings, such as this one from anarchist Nicolas Walter: "The biggest criminals are not burglars but bosses, not gangsters but rulers, not murderers but mass murderers."[16] Or this one from anarchist Stuart Christie: "Statist criminology treats of illegal crime, which is the least of society's serious problems and is treated as the greatest."[17] Aside from being erroneous by definition, because the law defines crimes and the state imposes law,[18] this condescending piffle trivializes popular fears of crime. People are afraid of the little criminals too, who might rob, rape or murder them. Price-fixing and securities fraud cause considerable harm, but they do not inspire fear. Some anarchists tend to sentimentalize criminals.[19]

An article by anarchist criminologist Larry F. Tifft, based on a 1983 address, sympathetically recounted Kropotkin's contributions to what Tifft then called "humanistic criminology." Kropotkin believed that universal sympathy, solidarity and economic equality, what Tifft calls (these are not Kropotkin's

---

(1868)," *No Gods, No Masters*, ed. Daniel Guérin, Oakland, CA: AK Press, 2005), 178.

15 Hippolyte Adolphe Taine, *The French Revolution*, trans. John Durand (New York: Peter Smith, 1931) 1:51. Cicero agreed. "On the Commonwealth," *On the Commonwealth and On the Laws*, ed. James E.G. Zetzel (Cambridge Cambridge University Press, 1999), 19.

16 Nicolas Walter, *About Anarchism* (updated ed.; London: Freedom Press, 2002), 76 (originally 1969).

17 Stuart Christie, "Publisher's Foreword," Larry Tifft & Dennis Sullivan, *The Struggle to Be Human: Crime, Criminology, and Anarchism* (Over the Water, Sanday, Orkney, UK: Cienfuegos Press, 1980), vii.

18 Bob Black, "An Anarchist Response to 'The Anarchist Response to Crime,'" *Defacing the Currency*, 195.

19 George Woodcock, *Anarchism: A History of Libertarian Ideas and Movements* (Cleveland, OH & New York: Meridian Books, 1965), 376.

words) a "feelings-based" or "needs-based criminology," offer a complete solution to the problem of crime.[20] Tifft offers more quotations from Kropotkin than I do, but they add nothing to mine. I am sure that between us, Tifft and I have identified all of Kropotkin's contributions to criminology. Tifft confirms by silence that I am right to conclude that Kropotkin had nothing serious to say about ordinary everyday interpersonal conflicts, and that he had nothing to say about dispute resolution processes. As is also true of Tifft himself. As far as I know, all that Kropotkin ever wrote on the subject was that "the causes of conflict being reduced in number, those conflicts which may still arise can be submitted to arbitration."[21] Very likely Kropotkin didn't know what arbitration is. Tifft may not know either.

James Guillaume, who shared with Michael Bakunin the honor of being expelled by the Marxists from the First International, wrote up a blueprint for anarchist society in 1876. It is unlikely, he wrote, that "theft and banditry" would persist once there is free access to the fruits of abundance. Like Kropotkin, who knew him, he believed that "Material well-being as well as the intellectual and moral uplift that will result from the truly humane training [!] afforded to all, will in any case make much rarer the sort of crimes that are the products of debauchery, anger, brutality or other vices." So no comrade will ever get drunk and disorderly? "Nevertheless, the taking of precautions"—in the form of a security "service" in which all workers will serve by rotation—will be instituted. But what if the workers don't want to play cop? The ones who do are the ones to worry about. There will be prisons too: a murderer "will have to be denied his freedom and kept in a special

---

20 Larry L. Tifft & Lois E. Stevenson, "Humanistic Criminology: Roots from Peter Kropotkin," *Journal of Sociology & Social Welfare* 12(3) (Sept. 2015): 488–520 (based on a lecture delivered in 1983, and not updated).

21 Peter Kropotkin, *Memoirs of a Revolutionist* (New York: Dover Books, 1971), 399 (originally 1899). Binding or non-binding arbitration? Presumably non-binding. Yet one modern anarchist endorses compulsory arbitration. Giovanni Baldelli, *Social Anarchism* (Chicago, IL & New York: Aldine-Atherton, 1971), 153–54.

establishment until such time as he can be returned to society."[22] Who will decide when that time has come? And who will keep the prisoner (or is it "patient") there?

But, according to Guillaume, the important thing is,

> even now we know that, thanks to the transformation which education will work upon character, crime will become very rare: criminals being now only aberrations, they are to be regarded as sick or demented: the issue of crime, which today occupies so many judges, lawyers and jailers, will diminish in social significance and become a simple entry under the philosophy of medicine.[23]

Later I will say what I think of the medical model of crime. For now I mention only that Guillaume, too, is oblivious to dispute resolution. Guillaume, bless his godless heart, anticipated every single cliché of anarchist criminology. The classical anarchists gave little thought to social order.[24] Their enemies think of little else.

In 2010, Professor Jeff Ferrell, after a twelve-year sabbatical away from anarchism, authored a brief entry on Kropotkin for *Fifty Key Thinkers in Criminology*. It's mostly just a capsule biography, with a very short summary of Kropotkin's critique of law and prisons.[25] It too reports nothing in Kropotkin about anarchist dispute resolution.

It's true that the fear of crime is way out of proportion to the incidence of the kinds of crimes which people fear, thanks to politicians and the media. Probably few people are

---

22 James Guillaume, "Ideas on Social Organization," in *No Gods, No Masters*, 260.

23 Ibid., 261. "Most anarchists wish, however," according to anarchist philosophy professor John P. Clark, "to retain the concept of crime as an injury to both individuals and to society as whole, which should therefore be a concern of all members of the community." *Max Stirner's Egoism* (London: Freedom Press, 1976), 83–84. "Most anarchists" have given the mater little thought. I know of none, aside from Clark, who have ever said anything like what Clark says here.

24 Michael Taylor, *Community, Anarchy and Liberty* (Cambridge: Cambridge University Press, 1982), 1.

25 Jeff Ferrell, "Peter Kropotkin (1842–1921)," in *Fifty Key Thinkers in Criminology*, ed. Keith Hayward, Shadd Maruna & Jayne Mooner (London & New York: Routledge, 2010), 30–36.

aware that crime in the United States has been declining for decades.[26] But there are still many crimes committed directly against persons and personal property. Outside of the 1%, most people have been victims of such crimes, or they know someone who has. Crime and the fear of crime are, like everything else in this society, unequally distributed. Women's fear of violence is justifiably high because the incidence of violence against women is high, especially in intimate relationships.[27] Anarchist rhetoric must ring more than usually hollow for rape victims and battered wives. Tell *them* that Monsanto and Walmart are greater criminals than their assailants.

Prince Kropotkin identified three categories of crimes: protection of property, protection of government and protection of persons.[28] Obviously, if the state is abolished, so are crimes against the state. "A good third of our laws," Kropotkin maintains—taxes, the organization of the military and the police, etc.—"have no other end than to maintain, patch up, and develop the administrative machine."[29] The estimate is completely

---

26 John G. Perry, "Challenging the Assumptions," in *Restorative Justice: Repairing Communities Through Restorative Justice* (Lanham, MD: American Correctional Association, 2002), 1. Even prison guards like Restorative Justice! But I am getting ahead of myself.

27 Larry L. Tifft, *Battering of Women: The Failure of Intervention and the Case for Prevention* (Boulder, CO: Westview Press, 1993), 171 n. 1; Jodi Lane *et al.*, *Fear of Crime in the United States: Causes, Consequences, and Contradictions* (Durham, NC: Carolina Academic Press, 2014), ch. 4 ("Gender: The Most Consistent Predictor of Fear of Crime"); Kristen Day, "Being Feared: Masculinity and Race in Public Space," in *Fear of Crime: Critical Voices in an Age of Anxiety*, ed. Murray Lee & Stephen Farrall (Abingdon, Oxon, England: Routledge-Cavendish, 2009), 82. Criminologists nowadays talk less about reducing crime, which they have no idea how to do, and more about reducing fear of crime by well-publicized gimmicks like Community Policing. They really have no idea how to do that either. There is presumably an optimal level of fear of crime—the point at which people take reasonable precautions without being paralyzed by fear. If academy-inspired police public relations campaigns lull people into a false sense of security, that is unconscionable. If what academics, police, politicians or journalists say terrorizes the population without cause, that too is unconscionable.

28 "Law and Authority," in *Kropotkin's Revolutionary Pamphlets*, 212.

29 Ibid., 214. Or as Kropotkin describes them: "It again is a complete arsenal of laws, decrees, ordinances, orders in council, and what not, all serving to protect the diverse forms of representative government, delegated or usurped, beneath which humanity is writhing."

arbitrary. I know one legal system—that of the United States—far better than Kropotkin knew any legal system, but I would not even try to make such an estimate. I think his is much too high. But it is also beside the point, if the point is the resolution of disputes in a modern anarchist society. When the government apparatus occasions disputes, they are often disputes within the governmental apparatus. People don't think that these kinds of laws are for their protection. They're not.

The major classical anarchist argument is that the protection of property is the major purpose of government (Kropotkin again):

> Half our laws,—the civil code in each country,—serves no other purpose than to maintain this appropriation [of the fruits of labor], this monopoly for the benefit of certain individuals against the whole of mankind. Three-fourths of the causes decided by the tribunal are nothing but quarrels between monopolists—two robbers disputing over their booty.[30]

Again the estimates are arbitrary. The description is ludicrously false with respect to the criminal law. The defendants and their victims who end up in court rarely fit the description of monopolists fighting over the spoils of exploitation. Probably no case, civil or criminal, ever addressed by a Neighborhood Justice Center fits the description. Some plaintiffs in civil cases (such as evictions and collection of consumer debts) might qualify as robbers and monopolists in some highly hyperbolic sense, but not the defendants in those cases. Divorces? Drug law prosecutions? Traffic violations? Antitrust prosecutions? Name changes? The enforcement of contracts, wills, powers of attorney and trust agreements? Courts do many things.[31] As some of these examples show, some of the law is facilitative, not directly restrictive or repressive.[32]

---

30 Ibid., 213.

31 Murray L. Schwartz, "The Other Things That Courts Do," *UCLA Law Rev.* 28 (1980-81): 438.

32 H.L.A. Hart, *The Concept of Law* (Oxford: at the Clarendon Press, 1961), 27–28;

Now it is old news that there is some correlation between poverty and crime. There's a link between crime rates and unemployment, and a stronger link between crime rates and economic inequality.[33] The poorest communities have the highest crime rates.[34] There is "an astonishingly linear relationship" between poverty and youth crime: "The worse the deprivation, the worse the crime."[35] Although overall crime rates in the United States have declined for decades, crime is concentrated in impoverished neighborhoods. The United States "allows up to 25 percent of its young people to grow up in extreme poverty, something that just isn't tolerated in other developed countries. It is from that population that most serious crime originates."[36]

However, poverty does not, for instance, explain white-collar crime. White-collar criminals are usually not poor and usually did not grow up in poverty.[37] The motive is often simply greed (and the rich are greedy too)—but some white collar workers embezzle as retaliation for perceived wrongs.[38] Presumably the anarchists would say that, by abolishing the class system and private property in the means of production—the more daring ones add: the abolition of money—they would

Malcolm Feeley, "The Concept of Laws in Social Science: A Critique and Notes on an Expanded View," *Law & Society Rev.* 10 (1976), 505–513; Marc Galanter, "Justice in Many Rooms: Courts, Private Ordering, and Indigenous Law," *J. Legal Pluralism* 19 (1981), 19.

33 Steven Jones, *Criminology* (3rd ed.; Oxford: Oxford University Press, 2006), 154–56.

34 Todd R. Clear & David R. Karp, *The Community Justice Ideal: Preventing Crime and Achieving Justice* (Boulder, CO: Westview Press, 1999), 113.

35 Elliott Currie, *Confronting Crime: An American Challenge* (New York: Pantheon Books, 1985), 146 (quoted), 148–51 (citing statistics from the United States, England and Denmark).

36 Alex S. Vitale, *The End of Policing* (London & New York: Verso, 2017), 171 (quoted); Robert Reiner, *Crime: The Mystery of the of the Common-Sense Concept* (Cambridge, England & Malden, MA, 2016), 4, 27, 55 & *passim*.

37 Edwin H. Sutherland, "White Collar Criminality," *Am. Sociolog. Rev.* 5 (1940): 1–12.

38 Donald R. Cressey, *Other People's Money: A Study in the Social Psychology of Embezzlement* (Glencoe, IL: The Free Press, 1953), 57–66; M.P. Baumgartner, "Social Control from Below," in *Towards a General Theory of Social Social Control*, 1: 309–11; Black, "'Wild Justice,'" 247.

eliminate the motive and the opportunities for white collar crime. Even that may not be completely true. For some people, crime is work. And for some of them, as for some other workers, their work, when well done, has intrinsic satisfaction: "some of the rewards of crime have to do with the satisfaction inherent in craftsmanship, for instance."[39] The urge to rob banks and crack safes is also a creative urge.

It is nonetheless possible in a society without private (or state) ownership of the means of production for there to be disputes about personal property, and for there to be disputes which, while basically personal in content, take the form of stealing or destroying property. An anarchist society would certainly have some property-related crimes if it retains, as the supposed anarchist Noam Chomsky advocates, "central financial institutions."[40] All that financial institutions do is move money around.[41] There is nothing better for stealing than money. Where there are banks, there is embezzlement, and bank robbers.

The anarchist criminologists (who are few and far between) do complain a lot about white collar and corporate crime and the crimes of the state.[42] These rarely prosecuted crimes do far more harm than do the street crimes which so excite politicians, journalists and almost all academic criminologists.[43] But the man on the street *is* afraid of street crime. Stronger enforcement of antitrust laws and environmental laws would do more for Josephine Average than any possible crackdown on street crime. But that would do nothing to reduce his fear of crimes against her person and property. The anarchists, and

---

39 Peter Letkemann, *Crime as Work* (Englewood Cliffs, NJ: Prentice-Hall, 1973), 159. This little-known but very interesting book is based on research on property crime career criminals, especially safecrackers and bank robbers.

40 *Chomsky on Anarchism*, ed. Barry Pateman (Edinburgh, Scotland & Oakland, CA: AK Press, 2005), 65; cf. Bob Black, "Chomsky on the Nod," *Defacing the Currency*, 132.

41 Black, "Chomsky on the Nod," 137.

42 *E.g.,* Tifft & Sullivan, *The Struggle to Be Human.*

43 Reiner, *Crime,* 55.

the anarchist criminologists, sympathize with the criminals, not the victims. Most people sympathize with the victims, not the criminals. This is not just a public relations problem for anarchists. It's a serious flaw in their doctrine.

Contemporary anarchist criminologists have added nothing to the classical arguments except a little postmodernist punk posturing. In 1998, Jeff Farrell, by then a tenured professor of sociology at Texas Christian University, wrote: "In promoting fluid and uncertain social relations, and attacking the sources of legal authority which stifle them, anarchist criminology aims its disrespectable gaze both high and low." It does not "bother pretending to incorporate reasoned or reasonable critiques of law and legal authority, either."[44] Then he does go on to bother to pretend to provide reasoned and reasonable critiques of law and social order. But the critiques are mediocre, unpersuasive and derivative. The only novelty is the bad-boy braggadocio. I doubt if Ferrell could get himself arrested. Ferrell's major substantive publication—it was probably what academics call his "tenure book"—is entitled *Crimes of Style: Urban Graffiti and the Politics of Criminality*.[45] Ferrell has produced a criminology of style—style without substance.

It was still possible, *in 1996*, in an anarchist anthology, to assert: "But what would a noncoercive society do with millions of living individuals thoroughly trained in antisocial violence, and more millions of immigrants with no democratic culture? The only answer is to reeducate them, turning prisons into schools for community rather than schools for more crime." Unfortunately, "Such an enterprise would be a standing invitation to moral authoritarianism, and it is scarcely imaginable

---

44 Jeff Farrell, "Against the Law: Anarchist Criminology," *Social Anarchism* 25 (1998) (unpaginated), available at www.socialanarchism.org & library.nothingness.org. An anarchist who can get tenure at Texas Christian University can't be much of an anarchist.

45 Boston, MA: Northeastern University Press, 1996. The sequel is more of the same: Jeff Ferrell, *Tearing Down the Streets: Adventures in Urban Anarchy* (NewYork & Hounsmills, Basingstoke, Hampshire, England: Palgrave, 2001).

that it could be managed along democratic lines."[46] No kidding. "Community" is something lived, not taught. The incarceration of millions and more millions has not been seen since the Holocaust and the Gulag, except in the contemporary United States, which presumably has a "democratic culture."

And so—I will inflict only one example on my patient readers—here is what anarcho-criminologists Larry Tifft & Dennis Sullivan had to say in 1980: "Within an environment of such freedom and social organization [*i.e.,* anarchy], anti-person, anti-nature, and anti-social acts need not be feared."[47] No reasonable man or woman believes this drivel.

The anarchists continue: If some people are still anti-social after the revolution, they must be crazy. We will cure them by gentle treatment.[48] Most of the mentally ill are harmless—Elliot Hughes is an exception[49]—even if they do make us uneasy. But the violent, acting-out kind of crazies aren't all going to be pacified by a revolution, or by being cuddled by sentimental saps. Violent people are usually *not* crazy. Crimes of passion are not committed mainly by maniacs. They are committed by ordinary men and women against other ordinary men and women with whom, usually, they are already involved, as the Vera Institute statistics showed (for instance, 50% for homicide, 83% for rape). The shocking fact about wife-beaters, who are numerous, is not that they are numerous, but that they are ordinary . . . "the attributes of men who

---

46 David Bouchier, "Hard Questions for Social Anarchists," in *Reinventing Anarchy, Again*, ed. Howard J. Ehrlich (Edinburgh, Scotland & San Francisco, CA: AK Press, 1996) (originally 1987), 117. Note the anti-immigrant prejudice of this "social anarchist"! In the United States, the crime rate is lower among immigrants than among native-born citizens.

47 Tifft & Sullivan, *The Struggle to Be Human,* 179.

48 *E.g.,* Walter, *About Anarchism*, 76.

49 In August 2015, at the Long Haul Infoshop in Berkeley where I was to speak, this psychotic, who is a ubiquitous haunter of Bay Area anarchist events, sucker-punched me, beating me into unconsciousness. The local anarchists who don't want anybody to ever call the police (I didn't) merely ejected the thug, and they have never retaliated. They will not tell me where to find him. Their cowardice and total lack of solidarity tend to confirm my suspicion that nobody acts less on anarchist principles than anarchists do.

batter women appear to be descriptive of men in the United States *generally*, rather than of men who batter women or of 'violent men' specifically."[50]

According to Nicolas Walter, "proper treatment of delinquency would be part of the health and education system, and would not become an institutionalized system of punishment."[51] But it would be part of an institutionalized system of health and education. Here's the same ploy as from Kropotkin: change the subject from social order to the villainy of punishment.[52] The same from Alex Comfort, a Freudian anarchist (I hope, the only one).[53]

As shown by my exemplary primitive societies, their dispute resolution processes are directed toward reconciliation, not punishment. At least they *have* dispute resolution processes. Alex Comfort does understand this much: "No society, however utopian, is likely to remove altogether the causes of delinquency.... The mechanism of restraint which operates most effectively is one which centralized institutional societies undermine—the interaction of public opinion and introjected social standards." He remarks—consistent with what I've said: "Our lack of experience of this force of public opinion in city aggregates makes us rather too ready to underestimate it. The ultimate sanctions of such a community, ostracism and excommunication, are probably more powerful than any institutional penalty."[54] People in fear of crime are supposed to accept this on faith? Because it is nothing but a statement of faith, a credo, dressed up in a little Freudian jargon ("introjected"). The effect of public opinion can be overestimated as well as underestimated.

For Dr. Comfort, there is nothing in between amorphous custom and "public opinion," on the one hand, and the

---

50 Tifft, *Battering of Women*, 12 (emphasis in the original).

51 Walter, *About Anarchism*, 77.

52 Kropotkin, "Law and Authority," 215–16.

53 Alex Comfort, *Authority and Delinquency in the Modern State: A Criminological Approach to the Problem of Power* (London: Routledge & Kegan Paul, 1950), 99–104.

54 Ibid., 101. Except that few "city aggregates" now approximate communities.

"ultimate sanctions," on the other. He has no conception of *dispute resolution processes*. No lay anarchist does, as far as I know. This even includes anarchist *anthropologists* such as Brian Morris, Jeff Farrell, Neal Keating and David Graeber. The only exception is Harold Barclay.[55] Anarcho-democrat Graeber has proposed nine "Tenets of a Non-existent Science" of anarchist anthropology.[56] None of them addresses dispute resolution, although, as we have seen, there is already a century of directly relevant ethnography and theory. Comfort actually is aware of primitive anarchist dispute resolution,[57] but for him anarchism is not a theory of social organization, it is an "attitude."[58] Graeber calls out his colleagues: "I think anthropologists should make common cause with [anarchists]. We have tools at our fingertips that could be of enormous importance for human freedom. Let's start taking some responsibility for it."[59] It is not too late for him to start.[60]

Well then, the anarchists go on, we will raise a new generation, unwarped by capitalism and the state. One of them says that this may take "a few generations."[61] Obviously we, the living, will not benefit from the paradise to be enjoyed by our remote descendants, if we have any remote descendants. Our children (we are assured) will, after anarchist tutelage, never exhibit aggression or hostility. With parents like that, I think they will. Hippie parents may have punk children who

---

55 *People Without Government: An Anthropology of Anarchism* (London: Kahn & Averill with Cienfuegos Press, 1982), 47–48 & *passim*.

56 David Graeber, *Fragments of an Anarchist Anthropology* (Chicago, IL: Prickly Paradigm Press, 2004), 65–76. Graeber, now deceased and formerly a professor at the London School of Economics, has himself remarked upon the small number of admitted, or acknowledged, anarchist academics. Ibid., 2–5.

57 He wrote the Preface for Barclay's *People Without Government*, 7–9.

58 Ibid., 9.

59 Ibid., 105.

60 It's too late now. He died in 2020.

61 Scott W., "The Anarchist Response to Crime," which may still be available at libcom.org, a little gang of maladorous anarcho-leftists in London. My rejoinder (suppressed by libcom) is Bob Black, "An Anarchist Response to 'The Anarchist Response to Crime,'" *Defacing the Currency*, 193–216.

have hipster children.[62] I doubt that Freud's Oedipus complex really exists, except occasionally. But someone might want to slay his father even if he didn't want to marry his mother. They might go on to be just good friends.

Some anarchists and utopians are noble, gentle souls, although I have rarely met one who was like that. But Robert Owen was like that. He was, wrote Engels, "a man of almost childlike, sublime simplicity, of character, and at the same time one of the few born leaders of men."[63] An industrialist—as was Engels!—Owen made major improvements in the working and living conditions of his textile workers, which (he reported) effected great improvements in their characters, despite the degraded conditions in which they had previously lived. All that is necessary, he concluded, is that the "rising generation" everywhere be socialized by and for the New System:

> In short, my friends, the New System is founded on principles which will enable mankind to *prevent*, in the rising generation, almost all, if not all the evils and miseries which we and our forefathers have experienced. A correct knowledge of human nature will be acquired; ignorance will be removed; the angry passions will be prevented from gaining any strength; charity and kindness will universally prevail; poverty will not be known; the interest of each individual will be in strict unison with the interest of every individual in the world.[64]

---

62 The anthropologist A.R. Radcliffe-Brown refers to the alternation of generations. Affectionate relations prevail between grandparents and grandchildren where they may not prevail between parents and children. A.R. Radcliffe-Brown, "Introduction," *African Systems of Kinship and Marriage*, ed. A.R. Radcliffe-Brown & Daryl Forde (London: Oxford University Press for the International African Institute, 1950), 1–85. I discovered this to obtain in my own family. My grandfather was a troublemaker and so am I. His son, who was my father, was conformist and servile. As an aside: in his younger days, Radcliffe-Brown was known as "Anarchy Brown." He knew Kropotkin. Alan Barnard, *History and Theory in Anthropology* (Cambridge: Cambridge University Press, 2000), 7; Graeber, *Fragments of an Anarchist Anthropology*, 16.

63 Frederick Engels, "Socialism: Utopian and Scientific," in Karl Marx & Frederick Engels, *Selected Works in One Volume* (New York: International Publishers, 1968), 407.

64 Robert Owen, "Address to the Inhabitants of New Lanark," *A New View of Society*

Although Engels implies that Owen was naïve, he wasn't too hard on him. There had to be utopian socialists before there could be scientific socialists, *i.e.,* Marx and himself. But the Marxist canon is as devoid of attention to dispute resolution as the anarchist canon is, even though Marx and Engels, like Kropotkin, actually came to know something about feud and its resolution in primitive societies. As fatuous as the Owen quotation is, with its Enlightenment optimism about education and psychology, Marxism has never improved on it and probably, surreptitiously, agrees with it.

The whole idea that interpersonal disputes are inherently anti-social or pathological is literally reactionary. It assumes an organic, holistic, totalizing community which supposedly existed in the distant past. That kind of community is a myth.[65] There's no reason to think that it ever existed at any time anywhere. As early as 1904, sociologist E.A. Ross waxed elegiac:

> Loose touch-and-go acquaintanceships take the place of those close and lasting attachments that form between neighbors that have lived, labored, and pleasured together. The power of money rends the community into classes incapable of feeling keenly with one another. . . . Everywhere we see the march of differentiation. Everywhere we see the local group—the parish, commune, neighborhood, or village—decaying, or else developing beyond the point of real community.[66]

In 1912, sociologist Charles Horton Cooley lamented the eclipse of American community:

> in our own life the intimacy of the neighborhood has been broken up by the growth of an intricate mesh of private contacts which leaves us strangers to people who live in the

---

and Other Writings, ed. Gregory Claes (London, England: Penguin Books, 1991), 127.

65 Alan Macfarlane, Sarah Harrison & Charles Jardin, *Reconstructing Historical Communities* (Cambridge: Cambridge University Press, 197), 1–4.

66 Edward Alsworth Ross, *Social Control: A Survey of the Foundations of Order* (New York: Macmillan, 1904), 433.

same house . . . diminishing our economic and spiritual community with our neighbors.[67]

Other laments have followed ever since.[68]

According to a painstaking accumulation of social indicators, since 1960, *all* measures of social and political connectedness in the United States—voting, church attendance, union membership, membership in organizations from the PTA to the NAACP to bowling leagues, and even weekend card games!—have declined dramatically, especially among those born after World War II, *i.e.*, effectively the entire current population. And the decline applies to *all* age, class, racial, religious, regional and educational categories.[69] Conflict has not been reduced, merely atomized.

Primitive societies like the ones I described earlier are as close to organic and holistic as you can get, yet they have disputes. Even among other social primates (which is all of them), cooperation can be promoted, not hindered, by a moderate level of aggression. This is even true of rats![70] Social conflict isn't always a bad thing. Even mainstream sociologists and anthropologists understand that.[71] Revolutionaries ought to understand that!

I think that there's some merit in the traditional arguments. Economic inequality is certainly an important cause of crime.

---

67 Quoted in *Roderick D. McKenzie on Human Ecology*, ed. Amos H. Hawley (Chicago, IL: University of Chicago Press, 1968), 72.

68 Maurice Stein, *The Eclipse of Community: An Interpretation of American Studies* (exp. ed.; Princeton, NJ: Princeton University Press, 1972) (originally 1960); Robert A. Nisbet, *Community and Power* (New York: Oxford University Press, 1962).

69 Robert D. Putnam, *Bowling Alone: The Collapse and Revival of American Community* (New York: Simon & Schuster, 2000).

70 De Waal, *Peacemaking among Primates*, 236.

71 Lewis Coser, *The Functions of Social Conflict* (New York: The Free Press, 1956); Georg Simmel, "Conflict," in *Conflict and the Web of Group-Affiliations* (New York: The Free Press, 1955), 11–123; Paul Bohannon, "Introduction," *Law and Warfare*, xi. As anthropologist Simon Roberts writes, "it should be clear that whatever the shared assumptions against which everyday life in a particular society may go on, we should not start out with the idea that peace and harmony necessarily represent a 'natural' state of things, disrupted only by occasional, pathological instances of trouble." *Order and Dispute*, 33–34.

And the state is itself a source of social disorder which may take the form of crime.[72] But anarchists shouldn't be thinking in terms of crime. They should be explaining that anarchy, the alternative to law and the state, is a voluntary form of society based on equality and mutual aid. The law is a crude and ineffective way to resolve conflicts between people.

More sophisticated than their economism and their moral indignation are anarchist critiques of the *nature* of law as a force for order, regardless of whose interests it serves and how badly it behaves. Law operates categorically, but "every case is a rule to itself." No two acts (crimes, if you will) are exactly the same. No two criminals are exactly the same. The consequences are never exactly the same. The victims, if any, are never exactly the same. But the laws are exactly the same. Law's equal justice is inherently unequal, and therefore inherently unjust. "As new cases occur, the law is perpetually found deficient." Then, either the judges distort the law to fit the facts, or distort the facts to fit the law, or the legislature enlarges the body of law and makes it more complicated. The result is that there is far more law than any judge or lawyer could ever know, and "the consequences of the infinitude of law is its uncertainty"—thereby, as anarchist William Godwin argued, defeating its purpose of regulating conduct.[73]

Anarchists believe, correctly—but only as an article of faith—that law does not provide much order, and that what order it does provide is often the wrong kind of order. They are unaware that even many social scientists acknowledge that most social order, such as it is, is even today maintained by nonstate—by *anarchist*—social relations.[74] That is also about

---

72 Black, "'Wild Justice,'" 233.

73 William Godwin, *An Enquiry Concerning Political Justice*, ed. Mark Philp (Oxford: Oxford University Press, 2013), 403–05 (originally 1793). "The rules of justice would be more clearly and effectually taught by an actual intercourse with human society unrestrained by the fetters of prepossession, than they can be by catechisms and codes." Ibid., 403.

74 Black, "An Anarchist Response," 235–36; Bob Black, "'Wild Justice,'"235. Donald Black writes that "the more we study law, indeed, the more we realize how little people really use it to handle their conflicts . . . " "Social Control as a Dependent Variable,"

as far as the more astute classical anarchists got in analyzing the problem of interpersonal conflict.[75] Modern expositions of anarchism go no further.[76]

Anarchists should stop pretending that their utopia will be one of universal harmony. It would not be.[77] When they talk like that, people dismiss them as naïve fools, and that's exactly what they are. They should acknowledge that there may always be disputes, but there are noncoercive, conciliatory ways of resolving most disputes in decentralized, egalitarian, anarchist societies. The only academic near-anarchist to recognize this is James C. Scott: "It is one thing to disagree utterly with Hobbes about the nature of society before the existence of the state (nasty, brutish, and short) and another to believe that the 'state of nature' was an unbroken landscape of communal property, cooperation, and peace."[78] Anarchists won't be able to explain any of this to other people until they understand it themselves. "Pathologically impelled action is a

in *Towards a General Theory of Social Control*, ed. Donald Black (Orlando, FL: Academic Press, 1984), 1:3, reprinted in Black, *Social Structure of Right and Wrong*, 1–26.

75 Peter Kropotkin, *Mutual Aid, A Factor of Evolution* (Garden City, NY: Dover Publications, 2006), 189 (originally published 1902); Alexander Berkman, *What Is Communist Anarchism?* (New York: Dover Publications, 1972), 186 (originally published 1929); Rudolph Rocker, *Anarcho-Syndicalism* (London: Pluto Press, 1999), 19 (originally 1938).

76 *E.g.*, Bob Black, "Anarchy 101," *Defacing the Currency*, 37–51; James Guillaume, "On Building the New Social Order," in *Bakunin on* Anarchism, ed. Sam Dolgoff (2nd ed.; Montreal, Canada: Black Rose Books, 1980), 371–72 (originally 1876); Nicolas Walter, *About Anarchism*; Ruth Kinna, *Anarchism: A Beginner's Guide* (Oxford: Oneworld Publications, 2005); Colin Ward, *Anarchism: A Very Short Introduction* (Oxford: Oxford University Press, 2004); Howard J. Ehrlich, Carol Ehrlich, David LeLeon, & Glenda Morris, "Questions and Answers About Anarchism," in *Reinventing Anarchy, Again*, 4–18.

77 One exception is David Graeber, *Fragments of an Anarchist Anthropology* (Chicago, IL: Prickly Paradigm Press, 2004), 30–31. However, his "anthropology that almost already does exist," 21–37, and his nine topics for anarchist anthropological investigation, 65–76, have nothing to say about dispute resolution except for a parenthetical mention of mediation. Graeber also believed that anarchism is perfected direct democracy, which I disputed in "Bob Black and David Graeber: An Unbridgeable Chasm," www.theanarchistlibrary/org.

78 James C. Scott, *Two Cheers for Anarchism* (Princeton, NJ & Oxford: Princeton University Press, 2012), xiv.

familiar concern after all; and any society must equip itself to cope with those who (as John Locke put it) act 'as a Lyon or a Tyger, one of those wild Savage Beasts with whom Men can have no Society nor Security.'"[79]

Disputes are universal. Third-party disputing processes are not universal, but they are very common in primitive societies. The more complex the society, the more likely it is to have processes of mediation or arbitration or adjudication, singly or in combination. A major determinant of their presence, and of which ones are present, is social scale and complexity. Anarchists are not in agreement about how complex their anarchist society should be. Like most classical anarchists, I am convinced that modern anarchy would have to be, as primitive anarchy always was, small in scale and radically decentralized. This implies a limit on how much of existing society it is possible or desirable to maintain. To me it's obvious that an anarchist society could not (and should not) preserve, and intensify, as Noam Chomsky claims,[80] much of modern industrial society, financial institutions, democracy and the rule of law. Rather, it has to approximate the *Gemeinschaft*, not the *Gesellschaft* ideal type.[81] Even if a pure community of this type has never existed, that is what we should try to approximate.

That society should, at its foundations, consist of face-to-face communities, was understood by Fourier, Owen, Kropotkin, Malatesta, Buber, Goodman, Perlman, Zerzan and many others. In such communities, negotiation and mediation would be, according to my arguments, viable, effective and anarchist. I don't give a damn about how primitive or how modern these societies are, if they are really anarchist.

---

79 Jeremy Waldron, "Rawls and the Social Minimum," *Liberal Rights*, 265, quoting John Locke, *Two Treatises of Government*, ed. Peter Laslett (Cambridge: Cambridge University Press, 1988), 274.

80 "The Relevance of Anarcho-Syndicalism (1976)," in *Chomsky on Anarchism*, ed. Barry Pateman (Oakland, CA & Edinburgh, Scotland: AK Press, 2005), 133, 136–37; Black, "Chomsky on the Nod," 128, 132–153 & *passim*.

81 Ferdinand Tönnies, *Community and Society* (New Brunswick, NJ & London: Transaction Publishers, 1988) (originally published 1887). Tönnies was not an anarchist, but he was a socialist.

It is a little more difficult to envisage what form dispute resolution would assume under anarcho-syndicalism. There, the formations at the base consist of self-managed workplace workers' councils, defined functionally, along with communes defined geographically. Certainly interpersonal disputes would arise in the workplace, as they often do now, although, no syndicalist has acknowledged this. I don't know if the elected comrade managers/militants would adjudicate these disputes themselves: that would not be very anarchist. They might instead add these disputes to the agenda (probably already overburdened) of the workplace assemblies, or a disputant might do that herself.

These meetings would be scheduled after work, if, under syndicalism, there ever *is* any time after work. Most workers in assembly will probably shun this obligation, because their relationship, if any, to the disputants is simplex, except maybe for a few pals and mates. A tribunal consisting of partisans of the parties, plus the managers, plus whatever militants like to go to meetings, seems to me to be inferior to any known dispute resolution process, except maybe trial by ordeal. Even trial by battle is no worse. In fact, it's a nonviolent version of the same thing.

What about mediation? Pure mediation requires a mediator accepted by both parties, but where neither disputant has to accept the settlement proposed by the mediator. Who might the mediator be? We have two precedents. In primitive societies, the mediator is someone who knows the disputants, in person or by reputation, or who at least has personal ties to the kin of both disputants. He is usually a person of greater wealth, or higher prestige, who can, if necessary, bring in his own kin and clients, added to the supporters of the cooperative disputant, against a recalcitrant party.

Under syndicalism, there might not be anybody with personal knowledge of both parties, or anyone who has cross-cutting ties with them, or with their friends or family. If there is somebody like that, he might not want to be a mediator, or he might not be good at mediation. Of course, under anarcho-syndicalism, there can be no differences in wealth. Might there be differences in prestige? Spanish anarchism had its stars. I imagine that there would be an anarchist egalitarian aversion to differences in prestige, such that a more respected, more prestigious person would be discouraged from conducting a mediation from which he might emerge with even more prestige (this is the main motivation for Ifugao mediators). Excellence and superiority are not syndicalist values. Neither is honor.

The other precedent is modern ADR, conducted by trained, specialized mediators and arbitrators—professionals—who have the power of the state behind them. I've provided evidence what's wrong with that. I hope that syndicalists would reject that, but I am not at all sure that they would. They are not, in principle, opposed to the division of labor in a complex industrial society, but they are ignorant of, or indifferent to some of its ramifications. If, as Cornelius Castoriadis and Noam Chomsky contend, the formulation of national economic plans is just another industry (the "plan factory"), with its own workers' collectives and council,[82] there might be no syndicalist objection to a self-organized cadre (I mean, "industry") of professional mediators. There is already an American Arbitration Association of professional arbitrators. But the anarcho-syndicalist fathers, like all other anarchists, have nothing to say about interpersonal dispute resolution.[83]

The first book by avowed anarchist criminologists, Larry Tifft & Mark Sullivan (published in 1980), only pauses briefly to endorse "direct justice" which "means no institutionalization of the resolving of conflict." That could be murder, dueling, feud, vigilantism and lynch mobs. Despite having social science Ph.Ds, Tifft & Sullivan are confused about what an institution is. If an institution means a permanent *organization*,

---

82 Black, "Chomsky on the Nod," 138–40.

83 There is nothing, for instance, in Rocker, *Anarcho-Syndicalism* or in Emile Pataud & Emile Pouget, *How We Shall Bring About the Revolution: Syndicalism and the Cooperative Commonwealth*, trans. Charlotte & Fredric Charles (London & Winchester, MA: Pluto Press, 1990) (originally 1909).

then there could be no anarchist institutionalization of justice, for institutionalized justice in that sense is necessarily the state, or part of the state. But organization might mean ad hoc disputing processes which people regularly resort to, like those I have described for several primitive societies. Tifft & Sullivan were, at that time, apparently not aware of the anthropological literature on disputing processes, which is inexcusable. But they were dimly aware of disputing processes like that, because they wrote: "These processes might include the airing of conflicts among mutually selected friends. Perhaps the persons in conflict could select a mediator."[84]

Perhaps! You never know. These two don't. Alas, we haven't heard the last from them. Read on.

---

84 Tifft & Sullivan, *The Struggle to Be Human*, 74.

8. "Restorative Justice"

"Restorative Justice" (RJ) is the latest in informal justice. (Actually, it was invented before NJCs, but it hasn't faded.) Once again, the leftist longing for peace, harmony and reconciliation has been turned against the left. Once again, the left—the *academic* left: nobody else has even heard of restorative justice—has been compromised, co-opted and duped.[1] Think of the criminal justice system as Lucy, the credulous academics as Charlie Brown, and the football as, successively, the juvenile court, small claims court, pretrial diversion, neighborhood justice centers, drug courts, and now Restorative Justice. Every time Charlie Brown runs up to kick the football, Lucy pulls it away at the last moment, and Charlie Brown ends up on his ass. And every time, he thinks that next time will be different. It's like voting.

The theoretical pioneer or, as he is often called, the "grandfather" of RJ is Howard Zehr, the Distinguished Professor of Restorative Justice at Eastern Mennonite University. From 1979 to 1996, he directed the Office on Crime and Justice under the Mennonite Central Committee.[2] He describes himself as "a white, middle-class male of European ancestry,

---

[1] Sharon Levrant, Francis T. Cullen, Betsy Fulton, & John F. Wozniak, "Reconsidering Restorative Justice: The Corruption of Benevolence Revisited?" *Crime & Delinquency* 45(1) (Jan. 1999): 3–27.

[2] Curriculum vita of Howard Zehr, available online at emu.edu/cjp/restorative-justice/howard-zehr-cv/CV.pdf.

a Christian, a Mennonite."[3] The Mennonite cult, whose background is Anabaptist, is pacifist and, in principle, like the Quakers, antinomian.[4] Obviously pacifists cannot collaborate with the state.[5] But that has not kept the Mennonites (or the Quakers) from collaborating with the state's criminal justice system: "Mennonites and Quakers, for example, often work with judges, lawyers, probation officers, and bureaucrats to create reform, while protesting the institutions they are working in."[6] Mennonites invented, and Quakers and Brethren (the "peace churches") promoted RJ in the late 1970s. It is a "faith-based" process.[7]

Without trying to make *too* much of it, there is much more religious influence and involvement in RJ than in the NCRs or other ADR programs. The methods of RJ—reconciliation through confession, repentance and forgiveness[8]—are overtly Christian. An Anglican bishop, introducing a book on RJ, explains: "This speaks to me of New Testament principles. . ."[9]

---

3 Howard Zehr, *The Little Book of Restorative Justice* (rev., updated ed.; New York: Good Books, 2015), 10. Since 2002, this book has sold over 110,000 copies. Ibid., 11.

4 Lawrence M. Sherman, "Two Protestant Ethics and the Spirit of Restoration," in *Restorative Justice and Civil Society*, ed. Heather Strang & John Braithwaite (Cambridge: Cambridge University Press, 2001), 35–51.

5 Gary Chartier, *Anarchy and Legal Order: Law and Politics for a Stateless Society* (New York & Cambridge: Cambridge University Press, 2013), 243.

6 Anthony J. Nocella II, "An Overview of the History and Theory of Transformative Justice," *Peace & Conflict Rev.* 6(1) (2011), 3. "Christianity certainly gave rise to the recent worldwide development of Restorative Justice programs and theory." Wayne Motley, review of Christopher Marshall, *Compassionate Justice* (2021), www.academia.edu.

7 Ibid., 3, 2; Zehr, *Little Book*, 18. Nocella's claim that "peacemaking criminology, rooted in a faith-based and holistic approach to crime and justice," was influenced by, among other "peace activists," Fred Hampton and Malcolm X, is dishonest and offensive. They were not peace activists. They had pride.

8 John Braithwaite, "Survey Article: Repentance Rituals and Restorative Justice," *J. of Political Philosophy* 8(1) (2000): 115–131; idem, *Shame, Crime, and Reintegration* (Cambridge: Cambridge University Press, 1989), 80–83. This isn't punishment? Cruel and unusual punishment, at that.

9 Stanley Booth-Clibborn, "Foreword to the First Edition," in Martin Wright, *Justice for Victims and Offenders: A Restorative Response to Crime* (2nd ed.; Winchester, England: Waterside Press, 1996), viii; see also Christopher D. Marshall, *Beyond Retribution: A New Testament Vision for Crime, Justice and Punishment* (Grand

Even secular RJ supporters mention the "evangelical" zeal of some of its advocates,[10] and their "self-righteousness."[11] According to the executive director of a South African RJ center: "Restorative justice is by its very nature spiritual"—and by spiritual he means, experiencing and relating to the supernatural.[12] But there is no such thing as the supernatural.

If RJ essentially involves recourse to the supernatural, it violates, in the United States, the Constitutional separation of church and state, if it is implemented by the state. Long before

---

Rapids, MI & Cambridge, UK: William B. Erdmans Pub., 2001); Michael L. Hadley, "Spiritual Foundations of Restorative Justice," in *Handbook of Restorative Justice*, ed. Dennis Sullivan & Larry Tifft (New York & London: Routledge, 2006), 174–187; Jack B. Hamlin, "Restorative Justice: An Answer to the Call of the Gospel of St. Mark for Service and Restoration," *International J. of Humanities & Social Sciences* 1(19) (2011): 277–285; Mark M. Umbreit, *Crime and Reconciliation: Creative Options for Victims and Offenders* (Nashville, TN: Abingdon Press, 1985), ch. 5 ("Biblical Justice").

10 *E.g.*, Carolyn Hoyle, "The Case for Restorative Justice," in Chris Cuneen & Carolyn Hoyle, *Debating Restorative Justice* (Oxford & Portland, OR: Hart Publishing, 2010), 3; Williams, *Victims of Crime and Community Justice*, 65.

11 Todd R. Clear, "Community Justice versus Restorative Justice: Contrasts in Family of Value," in *Handbook of Restorative Justice*, 471.

12 Michael Batley, "What Is the Appropriate Role of Spirituality in Restorative Justice?" in *Critical Issues in Restorative Justice*, ed. Howard Zehr & Barb Toews (Monsey, NY: Criminal Justice Press & Cullompton, Devon, UK: Willan Publishing, 2004), 371, 366. This idiot also asserts: "The supernatural always played a part in the indigenous understanding of justice." Ibid., 370. My accounts of the Plateau Tonga, Ifugao and Kpelle made no reference to the supernatural because it does *not* play any part in their disputing processes, nor does it in many other primitive societies. Ifugao religion, which is typically animist, consists of myths, rituals and magical techniques. It has no ethical content. The Ifugao rarely fear and never revere their many gods. R.W. Barton, *The Religion of the Ifugaos* ([Manasha, WI]: American Anthropological Ass'n [Memoirs of the American Anthropological Ass'n, no. 65], 1946). The Tikopia play jokes on their gods. Dorothy Lee, *Freedom and Culture* (Englewood Cliffs, NJ: Prentice-Hall, 1959), 35. Ancient religions, according to the classic account by William Robertson Smith, were devoid of moral ideas. *Lectures on the Religion of the Semites*, First Series (Edinburgh, Scotland: Black, 1889), 392. The Bushmen have an eastern and a western god who are not concerned with morality. Elizabeth Marshall Thomas, *The Old Way: A Story of the First People* (New York: Farrar Straus & Giroux, 2006), 258–59. Emile Durkheim was entirely incorrect to say that the word *morality* "is found in diverse forms in all societies." "Introduction to *Morality*," *Emile Durkheim on Institutional Analysis*, ed. & trans. Mark Traugott (Chicago, IL & London: University of Chicago Press, 1978), 199. In most African societies, the natives pay only intermittent attention to the spirit world. E.E. Evans-Pritchard, *Theories of Primitive Religion* (Oxford: Oxford University Press, 1965), 88. That would describe our society too.

I knew that what I was talking about was RJ, I wrote: "Obviously there are first amendment limitations on implementing this Gospel philosophy governmentally."[13] Obvious to me, but not obvious to the inventors of the Florida Faith- and Community-Based Delinquency Treatment Initiative in the state's Department of Juvenile Justice. Nor did the issue of the separation of church and state occur to the keenly trained minds of three college professors who talked up that program at an annual meeting of the Southern Sociology Society.[14]

RJ was invented by pacifists who were inspired by an ideology of harmony. They were, and are, religious zealots who abhor conflict: "for the Christian Mennonite movement it is the typically adversarial nature of criminal justice which has aroused critique."[15] RJ "practices contain or sanitize conflict in the reconciliation discourse, regarding it as an altogether destructive and unhealthy feature of human conduct."[16] But social conflict is inevitable, and not always harmful, and it has some useful social functions. We may have too much individual conflict but we don't have *enough* social conflict.[17] Conflict has always occurred in (and often between) anarchist societies. I've contended that probably it always will. Nonetheless, as we will see, contemporary anarchist academics are prominent exponents of RJ. They always get off at the wrong stop.

We saw that the NJCs made the tenuous and dubious claim to have been inspired by primitive disputing processes,

---

13 Black, "Forgotten Penological Purposes," 234 n. 42.

14 Ronald L. Akers, Jodi Lane & Lonn Lanza-Kaduce, "Faith-Based Mentoring and Restorative Justice: Overlapping Theoretical, Empirical and Philosophical Background," in *Restorative Justice: From Theory to Practice*, ed. Holly Ventura Miller (London: JAI Press, 2008), 139–165. As discussed below, RJ didn't go from theory to practice, but the other way around. It has never found a satisfactory theory.

15 Joanna Shapland, Gwen Robinson & Angela Sorsby, *Restorative Justice in Practice: Evaluating What Works for Victims and Offenders* (London & New York: Routledge, 2011), 7.

16 Bruce A. Arrigo, "Postmodernism's Challenges to Restorative Justice," in *Handbook of Restorative Justice*, 479. "Thus, fundamental to restorative justice is a commitment to order, homeostasis, and equilibrium." Ibid., 478.

17 Nils Christie, "Conflicts as Property," *British J. of Criminology* 17(1) (Jan. 1977), 1. Ironically, RJ boosters often cite this article.

those of the Kpelle for instance. We saw how false that was. RJ supporters also claim indigenous inspiration, but they make a bigger deal about it. They take it for granted that RJ is identical to indigenous procedures, which is an untenable assumption.[18] In the teeth of the well-known history, they say things like this: "Most analysts [?] trace the roots of RJ back to aboriginal practices that predate colonization by the West."[19] They locate the "foundations" of RJ in Navajo peacemaking and the African concept of *ubuntu*.[20] They also claim inspiration from the Maoris.[21] It's interesting that they *don't* mention the Kpelle, whose community moots are closer to RJ "circles" than to the NJCs supposedly inspired by the Kpelle moot.

In much the same way that the Mormon Church retroactively converts the dead, RJ devotees adopt indigenous ancestors. They do that because indigenous peoples are *chic*, and also to legitimate themselves with an origins myth,[22] which is something no religion can do without. But it's a pious fraud. We know very well that Mennonites invented RJ in the 1970s, from religious motives.[23] To claim that one or more white

---

18 Chris Cunneen, "What are the Implications of RJ's Use of Indigenous Traditions?" in *Critical Issues in Restorative Justice*, 346. There is the little matter of the state, for one thing. RJ is about as indigenous as chop suey or General Tso's chicken is Chinese. Iindigenous disputing processes, such as among the Ifugaos and Plateau Tonga, bear little resemblance to any version of RJ.

19 Clear, "Community Justice versus Restorative Justice: Contrasts in Family of Value," 463.

20 James W. Zion & Robert Yazzi, "Navajo Peacemaking: Original Dispute Resolution and a Life Way," *Handbook of Restorative Justice*, 151–160; Dirk J. Louw, "The African Concept of *Ubuntu* and Restorative Justice," *Handbook of Restorative Justice*, 161–173.

21 Zehr, *Little Book*, 18–19.

22 Kathleen Daly, "Restorative Justice: The Real Story," *Punishment & Society* 4(1) (Jan. 2002): 55–79; Douglas J. Sylvester, "Myth in Restorative Justice History," *Utah L. Rev.* (2003), 501–522; Chris Cunneen, "The Limits of Restorative Justice," in *Debating Restorative Justice*, 109–112.

23 "In Kitchener, Ontario, the first known restorative case involving two teenagers on a vandalism rampage in 1974 was responded to by a volunteer probation officer from the Mennonite Central Committee, Mark Yantzi." John P.J. Dussich, "Recovery and Restoration in Victim Assistance," in *The Promise of Restorative Justice*, 68. Dussich, after "twenty-nine years in the US Army's Military Police Corps, retir[ed] at the rank of colonel in 1993. For the past thirty-four years [as of 2010] he has been working

Mennonites in remote Kitchener, Ontario—led by a Mennonite *probation officer*, Mark Yantzi—"developed RJ out of aboriginal and Native American practices in North America and New Zealand,"[24] is preposterous. Whence came their ethnographic savvy? Probably not college. Eastern Mennonite University, where Howard Zehr is the grey eminence, doesn't even *have* an anthropology department. Christian theology cannot survive an encounter with either history or the ethnographic record. It's too bad that the Mennonites don't follow the example of their Amish cousins, who mind their own business, take care of their own, and leave the rest of the world alone.

I've referred to some of the claims made for the NJCs as extravagant. But they were modest compared to the claims made for RJ. NJCs were designed to deal with a specific range of disputes, especially those arising out of prior relationships where third parties were left out. There seemed to be some sort of theoretical rationale for NJCs, in the Vera Institute's *Felony Arrests*, and—more tenuously—in the writings of scholars like Richard Danzig and Frank Sander. Subsequent research tends to confirm that "the effectiveness of a dispute resolution method depends on its fit with the source of a particular conflict."[25] But for RJ, one size fits all. With one conspicuous exception, to be discussed, RJ has no theoretical or, indeed, rational basis. But the believers, the Arjays—as I shall

---

mostly in the field of criminology, specializing in victim services." "The Contributors," ibid., 258. The incident anticipates many of RJ's problematic features. The probation officer presented his plan to the court, which approved it *ex parte* (without notice to, and in the absence of the defendants and their counsel, if they had any). He then took the vandals to the houses of their many victims, where he forced them to apologize, and forced them to listen to the victims describe their losses and how they felt about them. (This was not their only punishment: they were compelled to pay restitution.) John Smith, "Righting the Relational Wrong," a speech delivered to the Canadian Parliament, May 6, 2014, available at www.arpacanada.com. Dr. Smith is a Professor of the Old Testament at the Canadian Reformed Theological Seminary., *i.e.*, a Calvinist. He then expatiated upon RJ's "Biblical Roots."

24 Nocella, "An Overview," 3 (quoted); Zehr, *Little Book*, 18.

25 John W. Budd, Alexander J.S. Colvin, & Dionne Pohler, "Advancing Dispute Resolution by Unpacking the Sources of Conflict," Sept. 30, 2017, at 1, available at www.academia.com.

sometimes refer to them[26]—promise the moon, as lunatics are wont to do. Their rhetoric is often a bizarre combination of solemnity and euphoria.

RJ has been advocated, and sometimes attempted, in "correctional settings" and schools, and for sex offenders, elder abuse, business conflicts, higher education disputes, teenage bullying, athletics, white collar crime, disaster management—even (a Howard Zehr initiative) in death penalty cases![27] RJ is a minor tweaking of alternative dispute resolution, yet it has messianic ambitions. Do I exaggerate? According to a Canadian law professor, RJ "is arguably the most significant development in criminal justice since the emergence of the nation state."[28]

"Restorative justice," as its grandfather (or godfather) explains, "is an approach to achieving justice that involves, to the extent possible, those who have a stake in a specific offence or harm to collectively identify and address harms, needs, and obligations in order to heal and put things as right as possible."[29] Another definition, often quoted, is by Tony Marshall, who sees it as "a process whereby all the parties with a stake in a particular offence come together to resolve collectively how to deal with the aftermath of the offence and its implication for the future."[30] But really there is no agreed-upon definition of RJ.[31] "Stake" is a capitalist metaphor, or a gambling metaphor.

---

26 No disrespect to the doo-wop band of that name, although, it was a lousy band (*e.g.,* "Good Night Sweetheart," on YouTube).

27 *The Promise of Restorative Justice: New Approaches for Criminal Justice and Beyond,* ed. John P.J. Dussich & Jill Schellenberg (Boulder, CO & London: Lynne Rienner Publishers, 2010). It was also pushed by neo-liberal Tony Blair's "New Labour": "Tough on crime, tough on the causes of crime," but he was only tough on crime (or rather, criminals). James Gilligan, *Preventing Violence* (New York: Thames & Hudson, 2001), 9–10. He was also tough on Iraqi civilians.

28 Bruce Archibald, "Why Restorative Justice Is Not Compulsory Compassion: Annalise Acorn's Labour of Love Lost," *Alberta L. Rev.* 42(3) (2005), 941.

29 Zehr, *Little Book,* 48.

30 Tony Marshall, "The Evolution of Restorative Justice in Britain," *European J. on Criminal Policy Research,* 4(4) (1996), 37.

31 Kathleen Daly, "The Limits of Restorative Justice," in *Handbook of Restorative Justice,* 135. The index to this anthology has 12 listings under "definitions of RJ."

By "those who have a stake in a specific offence," Zehr means primarily, *victims* and *criminals*—but he avoids those hard words: "A soft answer turneth away wrath: but grievous words stir up anger."[32] To "put things right" means to get right with God. The therapeutic purpose, which was present, but usually muted, in the NJCs, is in the forefront here. James Gibbs, Jr., viewed the Kpelle moot as therapeutic, and Richard Danzig, whom he inspired, called for a radical change of perspective, to "stop thinking of courts as adjudicators, and view them instead as parts of a therapeutic process aimed at conciliation of disputants or reintegration of deviants into society."[33] You can think anything you please, but courts *are* adjudicators. NJC advocates, in offering something for everybody, sometimes promised therapeutic benefits, but that was a minor theme. In RJ, as in the juvenile court movement, it's primary. RJ is "therapeutic jurisprudence." [34] At least the NJC pseudo-social movement was secular.

The medical model of interpersonal conflict has absolutely no validity. In treating disputants as patients, RJ demeans them. The "sick role," with its "element of dependency," is a subordinate role.[35] To speak of RJ facilitators as "healers of conflicts"[36] is pernicious nonsense, because conflicts are not injuries or diseases. This is the Therapeutic State, referring to "the ascendency of the medical model as the prevailing ideology of the modern welfare state [references omitted]."[37] The therapeutic model is inherently authoritarian, conservative, individualizing, isolating and atomizing. So it's not a way to

---

32 Proverbs 15:1 (KJV).

33 Danzig, "Towards the Creation of a Complementary, Decentralized System," 14–15.

34 Ruth Ana Strickland, *Restorative Justice* (New York: Peter Lang, 2004), 7–8.

35 Talcott Parsons, *The Social System* (new ed.; London: Routledge, 1991), 436–38 (originally 1951).

36 Marty Price, "Personalizing Crime: Mediation Produces Restorative Justice for Victims and Offenders," *Dispute Resolution Mag.* (Fall 2001) (unpaginated).

37 James J. Chriss, "Introduction," *Counseling and the Therapeutic State*, ed. James J. Chriss, "New York: Aldine de Gruyter, 1999), 5–6; see also Thomas Szasz, *The Therapeutic State: Psychiatry in the Mirror of Current Events* (Buffalo, NY: Prometheus Books, 1984).

"collectively address" problems. It licenses deep intrusions into personal life and the self.[38] Treating criminals as sick is at least as ominous as treating them as sinners, a point made by no less than Max Stirner:

> *Curative means* or *healing* is only the reverse side of *punishment*, the *theory of cure* runs parallel with the *theory of punishment*; if that latter sees in an action a sin against right, the former takes it for a sin of the man *against himself*, as a falling away from himself.[39]

This is an uncanny anticipation—and anticipatory repudiation—of therapeutic justice. It strikes right to the heart of the RJ claim that what Restorative Justice, at the end of the day, really restores, is nothing real. Rather, it is coerced compliance with what is posited to be the criminal's innate human nature, his better self. The Therapeutic State is a paternalistic and authoritarian state.[40]

To the limited extent that RJ may be popular, that reception owes a lot to the conservative moralistic political climate: "The search for community and for definitive moral responses to crime can be seen in the context of neo-liberal demands for greater individual responsibility and accountability."[41] The most ambitious attempt to apply the criminal law in a therapeutic way was the juvenile court. It was a failure. In the 1960s, anti-institutional challenges shook the helping bureaucracies:

---

38 "By bringing about profound changes at the most intimate levels of human experience, the state aims to integrate marginal citizens into the social mainstream. Further, resistance on their part will not be tolerated." Andrew J. Polsky, *The Rise of the Therapeutic State* (Princeton, NJ: Princeton University Press, 1991), 4.

39 Max Stirner, *The Ego and Its Own*, ed. David Leopold (Cambridge: Cambridge University Press, 1995), 213. "But the correct thing is that I regard it either as an action that *suits me,* that I treat it as my *property*, which I cherish or demolish. 'Crime' is treated inexorably, 'disease' with 'loving gentleness, compassion,' and the like." Ibid., 213–14. Except in Erewhon, where criminals receive treatment but the sick are punished. Samuel Butler, *Erewhon* (Hertfordshire, England: Wordsworth Editions Limited, 1996) (originally 1872).

40 Thomas Szasz, *The Medicalization of Everyday Life: Selected Essays* (Syracuse, NY: Syracuse University Press, 2007).

41 Cunneen, "Limits of Restorative Justice," 119.

the social workers, psychiatrists and psychotherapists. But they recovered their hegemony.[42] Restorative Justice is part of that counter-revolution.[43]

But, by what benevolent "process" are parties reconciled and traumas healed by RJ? By, among other devices, "victim/offender conferences," "family group conferences" and "sentencing circles." They are our old friend, *mediation*, metastasized.[44] They may bring in a few more participants than the victim and the criminal (the "microcommunity" or "community of care"). Enthusiasts for RJ are, as were enthusiasts for NJCs, academics and social control professionals—judges, elite lawyers, social workers, etc. (now joined by religious activists)—including the RJ paraprofessionals themselves. One would therefore expect them to be mindful of the NJC experience, not to mention the juvenile court experience.

But they are not. I have read only two RJ studies which referred to the NJCs—curiously, without calling them that. One reported that they were a great success,[45] citing none of the studies mentioned by Roman Tomasic or myself. The other acknowledged the finding of the Vera Institute's Brooklyn study, where there was a control group: the recidivism rates were the same. The article referred to the Brooklyn mediation program as "restorative justice," although it was never called that at the time.[46]

---

42 James L. Nolan, Jr., *Justifying the Welfare State at Century's End* (New York: New York University Press, 1998).

43 Annalise E. Acorn, *Compulsory Compassion: A Critique of Restorative Justice* (Vancouver, BC, Canada: UBC Press, 2004).

44 Paul McCold, "The Recent History of Restorative Justice: Mediation, Circles, and Conferencing," *Handbook of Restorative Justice*, 24–27; Mark S. Umbreit, Robert B. Coates, & Betty Vos, "Victim Offender Mediation: An Evolving Evidence-Based Practice," *Handbook of Restorative Justice*, 52–62; Christa Pelikan & Thomas Trenczek, "Victim Offender Mediation and Restorative Justice: The European Landscape," in *Handbook of Restorative Justice*, 82; Dennis Sullivan & Larry Tifft, *Restorative Justice: Healing the Foundations of Our Everyday Lives* (Monsey, NY: Willow Tree Press, 2001), 74. "Healing the foundations of our everyday lives" is a mixed metaphor and drooling idiocy.

45 McCold, "Recent History of Restorative Justice," 24–25.

46 Shapland, Robinson & Sorsby, *Restorative Justice in Practice*, 16–17.

The NJCs, as we have seen, had the initial support of almost everyone except the people of the communities where they were installed. Similarly, RJ boosters include "police officers, judges, schoolteachers, politicians, juvenile justice agencies, victim support groups, aboriginal elders, and mums and dads."[47] In other words, *authorities*. RJ enthusiasts have made many grandiose claims—but, that RJ is a response to popular demand, is not one of them. The American Bar Association, an early advocate of NJCs,[48] now publishes *Dispute Resolution Magazine*, which regularly features—alongside the self-congratulatory stories about community mediation centers which I've cited—self-congratulatory stories about restorative justice.[49] That RJ has *critics*[50] is rarely acknowledged by its real "stakeholders": law enforcement, some professors, liberal clergymen and the paraprofessional practitioners.

Although RJ is, I shall argue, even worse than the NJCs, it has been around even longer, and it is still around. The NJCs were an American phenomenon. RJ originated in Canada and it has spread to many parts of the world. It may still be spreading. An RJ website maintained by the Centre for Justice & Reconciliation, "operating within the Christian tradition," lists over 12,000 texts.[51] RJ is a—dare I say it?—godsend to academics who have to publish or perish. RJ is a very easy

---

47 Larry Johnstone & Daniel W. Van Ness, *Handbook of Restorative Justice* (Devon, UK: Willan Publishing, 2007), 76–77.

48 American Bar Association, *Report of the Pound Conference Follow-up Task Force* (Chicago, IL: American Bar Foundation, 1976).

49 *E.g.*, Marty Price, "Personalizing Crime: Mediation Produces Restorative Justice for Victims and Offenders," Dispute Resolution Magazine (Fall 2001) (unpaginated), available online at http://www.vorp.com.

50 *E.g.*, Daly, "Restorative Justice: The Real Story"; Acorn, *Compulsory Compassion*; Bruce A. Arrigo & Robert C. Schwehr, "Restoring Justice for Juveniles: A Critical Analysis of Victimoffender [sic] Mediation," *Justice Q.* 15(4) (1998): 629–666; Cunneen, "The Limitations of Restorative Justice," 101–187; Takagi & Shank, "Critique of Restorative Justice"; George Pavlich, *Governing Paradoxes of Restorative Justice* (London: Glasshouse Press, 2005).

51 http://restorativejustice.org; Cunneen, "The Limitations of Restorative Justice," 101. The Centre is a project of the Prison Fellowship International, which was founded by Watergate criminal Charles Colson after he got religion.

topic to write articles about. I've done it myself, although I didn't even know it at the time.[52] There are many, many books and articles: but, after 40 years, not much research. Mostly, Arjays write articles about each other's articles. Many other academics do the same.

Some of the claims for RJ (there are many more) are the same claims as were made for the NJCs. For each, I first cite to the corresponding NJC claim.

1. RJ is a voluntary, non-state alternative to the criminal justice (CJ) system.[53]

It is axiomatic for RJ that "participation by the one who has been harmed is entirely voluntary."[54] It is a non-state alternative to CJ. Crime victims who don't call the police or file complaints will rarely be drawn into a criminal prosecution. Lumping it is a non-state alternative to RJ only in the sense that it is no alternative at all. But if participation by the *offender* has to be entirely voluntary, then there exist almost no bona fide restorative justice programs.

For a subversive, non-state alternative to CJ—a new paradigm—RJ is strangely popular with the state. As early as 2001, "Virtually every [American] State [was] implementing restorative justice at state, regional, and local levels."[55] It is practiced in hundreds of prisons.[56] It is practiced in many schools.[57] It is endorsed by the United Nations[58] and has been implemented, in name at least, in many countries—including authoritarian states like Singapore, which allow nothing to escape state

---

52 Black, "Forgotten Penological Purposes."

53 Tomasic, "Mediation as an Alternative to Adjudication," 225–28.

54 Zehr, *Little Book*, 57 (quoted); Tifft & Sullivan, "Introduction: The Healing Dimension of Restorative Justice: A One-World Body," in *Handbook of Restorative Justice*, 2.

55 Price, "Personalizing Crime," n.p.

56 Nocella, "Overview," 4.

57 Vitale, *The End of Policing,* 71–72.

58 United Nations (July 27, 2000), *Basic Principles on the Use of Restorative Justice Programmes in Criminal Matters* (ESCO Res. 2000/14 U.N.Doc. E/2000.

control.[59] In New Zealand, the juvenile justice system has been, since 1989, based on RJ principles.[60] In California, "restorative justice and law enforcement personnel often interpenetrate": many probation officers are allowed to carry guns, they exchange information with police, and they ride along with police.[61] Worldwide, RJ is used far more for juveniles than for adults.[62] For them, if for anyone, there might be a place for its paternalism. Perhaps there is something infantilizing about RJ. Jesus taught that one must become as a child to enter into the Kingdom of Heaven.

Arjays are in hopeless denial about this touchy matter. We see something like this statement in most RJ books and articles: "Participation in restorative justice was entirely voluntary for victims and offenders"—and then, *on the same page*, we read: "In general, offenders proving uncontactable were relatively rare—not surprisingly, given that offenders were still in the criminal justice process either pre- or post-sentence."[63]

Here, then, is the first common feature of RJ and CJ. They are both court-annexed (in some countries, such as Australia, police-annexed[64]) and, as such, they are statist and coercive. For this, the Mennonites and Quakers are as sorry as the Walrus and the Carpenter.[65] All the other claimed benefits of

---

[59] Wing-Cheong Chan, "Family Conferencing for Juvenile Offenders: A Singaporean Case Study in Restorative Justice," *Asian J. of Criminology* 8(1) (March 2013): 1–23.

[60] Gabrielle Maxwell, Allison Morris & Hennessey Hayes, "Conferencing and Restorative Justice," in *Handbook of Restorative Justice*, 91–106.

[61] Paul Takagi & Gregory Shank, "Critique of Restorative Justice," *Social Justice* 31(3) (2004), 161.

[62] Thom Brooks, *Punishment* (London & New York: Routledge, 2013), 82; Mario Thomas Gaboury & Duane Ruth-Heffelbower, "Innovations in Correctional Settings," in *The Promise of Restorative Justice*, 16.

[63] Shapland, Robinson & Sorsby, *Restorative Justice in Practice*, 53.

[64] Ibid., 6 (this is the "Wagga Wagga model"). Also used in New Jersey. Margarita Zernova, *Restorative Justice: Ideals and Realities* (Aldershot, Hampshire, UK & Burlington, VT: Ashgate Publishing, 2007), 10–12.

[65] "I weep for you," the Walrus said:

> "I deeply sympathize."
> With sobs and tears he sorted out
> Those of the largest size,

RJ founder on this brute fact. State control of RJ is growing.[66] It is probably complete.

2. *RJ is therapeutic for victims, offenders, and others.*[67]

RJ is above all about *healing*, according to the definitions by Howard Zehr and many others.[68] RJ responds, not to crime *per se*, but to "harm." However, unless the harm is also a crime, state-annexed RJ can have no jurisdiction. If RJ is healing, whom does it heal? The "stakeholders" always include the offender, the victim and their immediate families. In cases involving juveniles, the parents are brought in—but the juvenile court has always done that.

By definition, because this is RJ—there has to be a harm— the victim has been harmed, physically, psychologically or financially. Restitution is often ordered in case of property crimes, but, it would be perverse to speak of "healing" the victim's finances. Besides, most offenders are unable to repair financial loss.[69] And there is nothing distinctively RJ about restitution. It's become a standard element in sentencing for property crimes. Physical harm is redressed by medical care,

---

    Holding his pocket-handkerchief
    Before his streaming eyes.
    "O Oysters," said the Carpenter,
    You've had a pleasant run!
    Shall we be trotting home again?"
    But answer there came none—
    And this was scarcely odd, because
    They'd eaten every one.

Lewis Carroll, "Through the Looking-Glass," *The Annotated Alice: The Definitive Version* (New York & London: W.W. Norton & Company, 2000), 187–88.

66 "Carolyn Boyes-Watson, "What Are the Implications of the Growing State Involvement in Restorative Justice?" in *Critical Issues in Restorative Justice*, 215–24.

67 Danzig, "Towards the Creation of a Complementary, Decentralized System," 14–15 (NJCs).

68 *E.g.,* Zehr, *Little Book*, 48 & *passim*; Susan Sharpe, *Restorative Justice: A Vision for Healing and Change* (Edmonton, Alberta, Canada: Mediation and Restorative Justice Centre, 1998).

69 Martin Wright, *Justice for Victims and Offenders: A Restorative Response to Crime* (2nd ed.; Winchester, UK: Waterside Press, 1996), 151; Black, "An Anarchist Response to 'The Anarchist Response to Crime,'" 206.

not in an encounter group. So RJ's healing claims really boil down to the provision of psychotherapy. However, "there are more effective means of assisting the process of emotional catharsis and addressing mental health issues than reliance on the criminal justice system."[70] And I have suggested: "For the justice system, doing justice is more important than administering therapy."[71]

The meaning of "harm" to a victim, beyond violence to the person and trespass to property, is highly problematic.

Psychiatric, psychological and social services are available to victims, independently of RJ. Since the 1970s, there have been significant support services available to the victims of crime. It's always possible to say that such programs are inadequate. Has there ever been a social services program which didn't want more money? RJ wants more money too: "A common theme in the restorative justice community throughout the world is the lack of resources for programs at all levels."[72] Unlike RJ, which is a one-shot fix, these programs at least offer services over a relatively long-term basis. There's a "natural disconnect" between RJ and victim services.[73]

The typical RJ process, such as victim-offender reconciliation programs (VORPs), after some behind-the-scenes manipulation of the parties by the "facilitator" or "convenor," culminates in a single meeting of stakeholders. This fact alone renders the strident claims for success and satisfaction dubious. NJC mediation was a more protracted process, but as we have seen, its claims for success were also dubious. Successful mediation follows "essentially a *model of overlapping phases*

---

70 Jonathan Doak, "Honing the Stone: Refining Restorative Justice as a Vehicle for Emotional Redress," *Contemporary Justice Rev.* 14(4) (2011), 439.

71 Black, "Forgotten Penological Purposes," 230.

72 Vernon E. Yantzi, "What is the Role of the State in Restorative Justice?" in *Critical Issues in Restorative Justice*, 193. Dr. Yantzi, a professor at Eastern Mennonite University, is almost certainly related to Mark Yantzi, the Mennonite probation officer who originated victim/offender mediation in Canada. The Mennonites are very inbred.

73 Dussich, "Recovery and Restoration," 69–70 (quoted); Herman, "Is Restorative Justice Possible Without a Parallel System for Victims?" 77–78.

in which each phase opens the way to a succeeding one in a progression toward settlement. The phases are distinguished by the nature and content of the information exchanged and the concomitant learning and by the degree of coordination involved."[74] That was how mediation was conducted in unhurried societies such as the Plateau Tonga and the Ifugao. But that's not modern RJ. Modern societies are not unhurried.

RJ literature is loaded with moving anecdotes of "closure" for victims, and of criminals seeing the light[75]—the blinding light, such as St. Paul saw on the Damascus road. In one infamous, oft-quoted anecdote, it was the *victim*, who really *was* blinded, while in custody, by a South African police officer, and whose sight was (metaphorically) restored by the opportunity to tell his story to a Truth and Reconciliation Commission.[76]

I am so hard-hearted as to shed no tears of joy over these miracles, possibly because I don't believe in miracles. I am sure the Arjays shed tears as sincerely as did the Walrus and the Carpenter.[77] But I have not found a single *case*, documented by psychologists or psychiatrists or psychiatric social workers, of RJ effecting personality changes in anybody. RJ is much less like therapy than theatre—the theatre of the absurd, or melodrama.

If victim healing is dubious, offender healing is scandalous. As we have seen, the real focus of most RJ programs is on rehabilitating the criminal, not healing the victim. The only

---

74 Gulliver, "On Mediators," 22. Here is yet another reason why the Kpelle moot is not mediation.

75 *E.g.*, Howard Zehr, *Transcending: Reflections of Crime Victims: Portraits and Interviews* (Intercourse, PA: Good Books, 2001).

76 Acorn, *Compulsory Compassion*, 71. I will not burden my overlong discourse with the story about how RJ is the ideology behind truth and reconciliation commissions in various countries coming to terms with the legacy of their previous repressive regimes. That may have been politically expedient, even necessary, but the rationale is even feebler than for RJ in ordinary criminal cases. Stuart Wilson, "The Myth of Restorative Justice: Truth, Reconciliation and the Ethics of Amnesty," *South African J. of Human Rights* 17 (2001): 531–562.

77 "'I like the Walrus best,' said Alice: 'because he was a *little* sorry for the poor oysters.' 'He ate more than the Carpenter, though,' said Tweedledee." Carroll, *Through the Looking-Glass*, 187–88.

"harm" to a convicted criminal is criminal punishment. Naturally he would like to avoid that. The lion would rather eat the lamb than lie down with him, but, he might prefer lying down with the lamb to being caged. But why should the lamb lie down with the lion? Nonetheless, that is the idyllic illustration on the cover of Tifft & Sullivan's *Restorative Justice*. A child is petting the lamb. A dove of peace observes from a tree branch. I'm not making this stuff up! [78]

Most people adhere, more or less consciously, to the "retribution" theory of criminal punishment, which is also currently popular among academics, who always bend with the winds, and bend over for the state. The scriptures of the Western religions—Judaism, Christianity and Islam—espouse it, and demand it. Most people think that, in general, criminals should get their just deserts, which will probably harm the criminals—that's the *point*. I don't endorse this point of view. I merely recognize its popularity. For the pacifist founders of RJ, retribution is anathema (another religious word), and RJ is the alternative. Criminals too, they say, need to be healed. One reason RJ is less popular with victims than with offenders is that victims may be offended when "the real criminals" are treated as victims too. They might be outraged to hear an Arjay saying "that most street criminals—the 'bad guys' in our justice system—are in fact victims themselves."[79] So what? Any victim of crime knows better than the RJ academic who babbled: "Crime does not exist."[80] For RJ, we are all victims. An ardent academic Arjay admits:

> Although the principles of restorative justice profess that

---

[78] The Bible quotation is actually different, and a little more elaborate, than is commonly assumed: "The wolf shall also dwell with the lamb, and the leopard shall lie down with the kid; and the calf and the young lion and the fatling together; and a little child shall lead them." Isaiah 11:6 (KJV). Not all of this menagerie is in the illustration. I don't know if Tifft & Sullivan are Protestants, but many of their RJ colleagues are, and they might have done some fact checking.

[79] Bonnie Price Lofton, "Does Restorative Justice Challenge System Injustices?" in *Critical Issues in Restorative Justice,* 384.

[80] Nils Christie, *A Suitable Amount of Crime* (Oxford: Oxford University Press, 2001), 123.

it is for both offenders and victims, the reality is that the majority of programs are predominantly being used for offender rehabilitation. For the most part, victims are still being neglected by most practitioners in the countries where restorative justice is used.[81]

Victims are not merely neglected by RJ practitioners: they are being used. And they are being had.

Now I can agree with this: "There is not a simple dichotomy between a homogeneous aggregation of law-abiding citizens and a homogeneous aggregation of law violators."[82] It's a good thing for RJ that victims haven't read the RJ academic literature, where they might read that

> victims are not necessarily the "good" in opposition to the offender's "bad." ... [T]his position serves to remind us that whilst crime does impact upon [sic] people's lives, victims of crime are people too. So by implication, in this regard, it makes little sense to talk of people as victims or offenders, or indeed victims or survivors. They are people, and people need to feel OK about themselves and sometimes need some help and support to achieve that.[83]

For victims, if not for sociology professors, it makes perfect sense to talk of people as victims or offenders. Their common personhood did not prevent the offenders from victimizing their victims. Maybe some people should *not* "feel OK about themselves," because some people are *not* OK.

---

81 Dussich, "Recovery and Restoration," 68; see also Susan Herman, "Is Restorative Justice Possible Without a Parallel System for Victims?" in *Critical Issues in Restorative Justice*, 77.

82 Joseph F. Donnermeyer & Walter S. DeKeseredy, *Rural Criminology* (London & New York: Rutledge, 2014), 66.

83 Sandra Walklate, "Changing Boundaries of the 'Victim,'" *Handbook of Restorative Justice*, 283–84. Why is "Victim" in quotation marks? Nobody is being quoted. "Quotation marks are to be rejected as an ironic device. For they exempt the writer from the spirit whose claim is inherent in irony, and they violate the very concept of irony by separating it from the matter at hand and presenting a predetermined judgment on the subject." Theodor W. Adorno, "Quotation Marks," *The Antioch Review* (Summer 1990), 303, quoted in Bob Black, *Anarchy after Leftism* (Columbia, MO: C.A.L. Press, 1997), 38.

Criminals don't usually need to be healed, because criminals, like victims, aren't usually sick. If they are, that has little to do with their criminality. Possibly juvenile delinquents, who are still growing up, should be treated therapeutically—at first, anyway. For the Arjays, a crime is an opportunity for ministration. For them, in accordance with their sickly Christian morality,[84] the criminal is a sheep gone astray. They wallow in bathos. They rejoice in it. Arjays are leper lickers.

In the parable of the Prodigal Son, the whoring, wastrel son leaves home while the dutiful son remains to serve his father. When the Prodigal, whose money has run out, drags his sorry ass back home, the patriarch rejoices, and he sacrifices the fatted calf: "For this my son was dead, and is alive again; he was lost, and is found. And they began to be merry."[85]

But not everybody began to be merry. The dutiful, obedient son "was angry, and would not go in: therefore came his father out, and entreated him." The father told him, in effect: you I can take for granted. But your brother needs to be (this is RJ jargon, not the Bible) "reintegrated."[86] Had they all been brought together in a "family circle," facilitated by a holy man—that would be RJ. When Christianity isn't advocating rendering unto Caesar, and explaining that the powers that be are ordained of God, it occasionally privileges the wrongdoer. Where would Christianity be without sin?

Curiously, these Christians never discuss crime in terms of good and evil, although that is historically their stock in trade. Like Father Flanagan of Boys Town, they believe that there is no such thing as a bad boy—or girl, or man, or woman. Often,

---

[84] "From the start, the Christian faith is a sacrifice: a sacrifice of all freedom, all pride, all self-confidence of the spirit; at the same time, enslavement and self-mockery, self-mutilation." Friedrich Nietzsche, "Beyond Good and Evil," *Basic Writings of Nietzsche*, trans. & ed. Walter Kauffman (New York: The Modern Library, 1968), 250. For Nietzsche, "man's 'sinfulness' is not a fact, but merely the interpretation of a fact, namely of physiological depression—the latter viewed in a religio-moral perspective that is no longer binding on us." "On the Genealogy of Morals," in ibid., 565.

[85] Luke 15: 11–27 (quotation at 11: 24) (KJV).

[86] Luke 15: 28–32 (KJV).

victims don't share that opinion. They often perceive RJ as favoring criminals over victims.[87] They often consider offender apologies to be insincere.[88] In one study which emphasized the apology ceremony, the juvenile delinquents, when later asked why they apologized, "27% said they did not feel sorry but thought they'd get off more easily, 39% said to make their family feel better, and a similar percent said they were pushed into it."[89] In other words, what they were sorry about was getting caught.

It's all too likely, also, that "restorative justice projects might report victim expression of forgiveness (as a performative action) that may not equate with a change in sentiment for themselves as individuals."[90] Probably "that which is spoken in the mediation session often is unwittingly scripted."[91] Maybe not so *unwittingly* at that. What makes excuses acceptable is not so much that they are true or sincere but that they follow a culturally accepted script.[92] The sub-professional facilitators write the script. Where the criminal has made a public show of his apology, the victim comes under pressure to accept the apology—or claim to—because she knows that's what the RJ paraprofessional gently, but firmly

---

87 There's a detail in the story which the preachers never mention: "Son, thou art ever with me, and all that I have is thine." Luke 15: 31.

88 Zernova, *Restorative Justice*, 11; Daly, "Limits of Restorative Justice," 139–40; Brooks, *Punishment*, 82. In one study, most victims accepted the offender's apology—but barely one third of offenders offered apologies. Mandeek K. Dhami, "Offer and Acceptance of Apology in Victim-Offender Mediation," *Critical Criminology* 20 (2012): 45–60. One-third x one-third works out to less than 11%.

89 Daly, "Limits of Restorative Justice," 140.

90 Ross McGarry & Sandra Walklake, *Victims: Trauma, Testimony and Justice* (London & New York: Routledge, 2015), 137–38. I will not explain why the philosophical term "performative," introduced by J.L. Austin, is meaningless here. Cf. J.L. Austin, "Performative Utterances," *Philosophical Papers*, ed. J.O. Urmson & G.J. Warnock (3rd ed.; Oxford: Oxford University Press, 1979), 233–252 (originally 1956).

91 Arrigo,"Postmodernism's Challenges to Restorative Justice," 478.

92 Ken-ichi Ohbuchi, "A Social Psychological Analysis of Accounts: Toward a Universal Model of Giving and Receiving Accounts," *Japanese Apology Across Disciplines*, ed. Naomi Sugimoto (Commack, NY: Commack Science Publishers, 1999), 28–29.

expects from her.[93] It's what the victim is there for. It will get her out of the room faster.

I describe the victim as *she* and *her* deliberately. In the kinds of cases relegated to RJ, much more often than not the victim is female, and much more often than not, the perpetrator is male. Often these are crimes of violence. Feminists have long criticized the unresponsiveness of the criminal justice system to female victims of male violence. They demanded that retributive justice be applied to these violent men.[94] Just when the feminists were starting to get somewhere with policymakers, along came the long lingering RJ policy fad whose solicitude is more for the (usually) male criminal than for the (usually) female victim.

Obviously RJ demands much more from the victim than from the criminal, although for almost anybody not ensorcelled by RJ ideology, it should usually be the other way around. Apology is a lot easier than forgiveness. And it's a lot easier to fake. Calling this "justice" does not pass the laugh test. In the unlikely event that I were a feminist, I would be even more suspicious of Restorative Justice than some feminists already are.

In a way, RJ could be passed off as feminist. If feminism is associated with supposedly essential(ist) female attributes such as caring more about relationships than rights, being more cooperative than competitive, being a good listener, and being more conciliatory than vindictive,[95] then there is something warm, nurturing, amniotic and feminist about RJ. "It is the feminine, Native American and African elements of

---

93 "While restorative justice insists that the victim's participation be wholly voluntary (it would of course be unconscionable if it were coerced), its insistence on consent does not let restorative justice off the hook of having to answer for the ethics of the tactics it uses to secure the victim's participation." Acorn, *Compulsory Compassion*, 70. "[R]estorative justice uses talk of healing as a means of enticing victims to participate." Ibid., 71.

94 Ibid., 3.

95 Carol Gilligan, *In a Different Voice: Psychological Theory and Women's Development* (Cambridge, MA: Harvard University Press, 1993) (originally published 1982). I am always skeptical of conclusions based entirely on interviews with college students.

our current [white male] leaders' souls," say some RJ women, "and their unity with all of us that are being expressed in their restorative justice work."[96] There are feminist Arjays making this argument.[97] There are many feminist Arjays in the academy. The ideal or idealized woman, on this account, is also the ideal or idealized victim. She's a pushover. She is predisposed to play the victim role in RJ dramas. She is the leading lady there.

But feminists—regardless to what extent they endorse or reject this unfortunate ideal type or stereotype—have correctly foregrounded the criminal justice system as a major site of the oppression of women, by their relentless critique of the way it deals with violence against women. For abused women they demand, of course, as a first priority, protection, which nobody openly opposes. But they go on to criticize, comprehensively, how women victims of crime are dealt with by the criminal justice system. The brute fact is that "the demographics of restorative justice on the question of who is required to learn love of their victimizers will prove no exception to this rule: Women victims of domestic violence, sexual assault, and other crime will be overrepresented in the pool of victim participants in restorative justice programs."[98] Men will be overrepresented in the pool of victimizers.

Do feminists want men (any men) who rape or batter women to be treated the way violent male criminals who are poor, young and black are treated? I'm curious to hear an answer to that question.[99] For now, I will confine myself to

---

96 Barbara E. Reye, "How Do Culture, Class and Gender Affect the Practice of Restorative Justice? (Part 2)," in *Critical Issues in Restorative Justice*, 336.

97 *E.g.*, ibid.; Emily Gaardner & Lois Presser, "A Feminist Vision of Justice? The Problems and Possibilities of Restorative Justice for Girls and Women," in *Handbook of Restorative Justice*, 483–494.

98 Acorn, *Compulsory Compassion*, 44.

99 "Feminist criminology has prospered by focusing on the light of women—women victims and potential victims and women offenders—and instead [have] avoided the largely more pressing task of bringing feminist analyses to bear on the old penological question of the rehabilitation of (largely male) offenders, especially violent offenders." Mariana Valverde, "Analysing Punishment: Scope and Scale," *Theoretical Criminology* 16(2) (2012), 248.

noticing that RJ is vulnerable to the feminist critique. RJ is better for male criminals than for female victims.[100] I, personally, don't want anybody to be mistreated, except my personal enemies, my political enemies, my class enemies, my . . . —I'll have to walk that back. I don't necessarily sorrow if my enemies are mistreated that way, if anybody is to be treated that way. Some feminists apparently feel as I do. They are no exception to the widespread popularity of retributive justice.

Academic advocates of RJ, many of them women, are very defensive when it comes to RJ in sexual and domestic violence cases. There, its use is "highly controversial."[101] But about all they can say is that the conventional criminal justice system is just as bad, if not worse.[102] Actually, it might be better. There is no evidence that it's not. A "new paradigm," or even a mere transformative reform, has to make a better showing than that. RJ has had plenty of time to do so.

In fact, offender apologies often *are* insincere. Coerced apologies are insincere.[103] What parent doesn't know that? ("Say you're sorry"). What former child doesn't remember that? This alone undermines claims that RJ is therapeutic for victims. As one researcher put it: "A rather high level of satisfaction was reported among participants, *except victims*." 50% of victim participants expressed satisfaction; 25% were indifferent; and 25% of victims felt worse.[104] A number of studies find, not surprisingly, that victims are the least satisfied participants in RJ.[105] The evidence suggests scrapping RJ, which, of course, will not happen. The RJ industry has too many stakeholders.

In return for the criminal's show of remorse and repentance, which is degrading, the victim is expected to put on a

---

100 Cunneen, "Limitations of Restorative Justice," 148–154.

101 Nicole Westmarland, *Violence Against Women: Criminological Perspectives on Male Violence* (London: Routledge, 2015), 100–101.

102 Hoyle, "The Case for Restorative Justice," 77–78.

103 Thom Brooks, *Punishment* (London & New York: Routledge, 2013), 82.

104 Zernova, *Restorative Justice*, 11 (emphasis added).

105 Acorn, *Compulsory Compassion*, 70.

show of forgiveness and conciliation.[106] The greatest beneficiaries of RJ are surely the jive hustlers: the glib, fast-talking con-men. The inarticulate—and they will include some women, and many juveniles, and more generally the lower orders—may not be good at telling their stories or voicing remorse in a way the victims recognize or which follows the RJ script. The Arjays—this shows how, as Christians, heretical they are—posit that human nature is innately good. For them, "restorative" refers, not to restoring the status quo, in relationships for example (where that may not be possible or desirable)—it refers to "restoring" people to be the best in themselves, the best they can be.[107] It's not the restoration of anything that was ever there in the first place. "Restorative" is a misnomer and "restorative justice" is a pretext. Self-realization, spiritual transformation, the warm glow of fellow-feeling—you get all that, just by attending a conference.[108] Who knew that it was that easy? Victims of crime don't know how lucky they are.

Crime victims have justifiably complained about their neglect by the criminal justice system. Exploiting their resentment, designing politicians legislated "rights" for them.[109] This began in the 1970s, shortly before the ancient practice of Restorative Justice was invented. Victims received the right to be informed of developments in the case. They received the right to submit Victim Impact Statements to the court, and sometimes to address the court in person, about the impact

---

106 "*Against Remorse*— . . . After all, what is the good of it! No deed can be undone by being regretted; no more than by being 'forgiven' or 'atoned for.' One would have to be a theologian to believe in a power that annuls guilt: we immoralists prefer not to believe in 'guilt.'" Friedrich Nietzsche, *The Will to Power*, ed. Walter Kaufmann, trans. Walter Kaufmann & R.J. Hollingdale (New York: Vintage Books, 1968), 136.

107 Human nature—the biggest lie in theology, moral philosophy, and libero-conservative ideology—I have debunked elsewhere. Black, "Chomsky on the Nod," 103–117 & *passim*; Black, *Nightmares of Reason*, ch. 9.

108 "It may be unreasonable to expect that an hour-and-a-half restorative encounter would turn around what are quite often life-time problems." Zernova, *Restorative Justice*, 33.

109 Robert Elias, *The Politics of Victimization: Victims, Victimology, and Human Rights* (New York: Oxford University Press, 1986).

of the crime on their lives. Conservatives love victims' rights because they hate criminals. Liberals love victims' rights because they love victims. Versions of victims' rights bills were soon enacted in almost all states.[110] But, as I've observed: "It is in reform movements which seem to promise something for everybody that the apparent accord on a program is likely to mask disagreement on objectives."[111]

That lesson has direct application to RJ, the brave new paradigm, which is of vast international scope, which is endorsed by left and right, by police and criminals, by college professors and Christian pacifists, by anarchists and the U.S. Department of Justice, and by the United Nations and the American Bar Association. And by Noam Chomsky and Bishop Desmond Tutu. Obviously there is something deeply wrong here. What's wrong with this picture?

What's wrong is who *isn't* in the picture: the victim. Victims' Rights (VR) legislation makes much more modest demands on the time and the emotions of victims than does RJ. VR doesn't mandate a victim's face to face public confrontation with the criminal, or her participation in a repentance/forgiveness ritual. Surely this is an experience which many victims will experience as an annoying waste of time, and which some will experience as a second victimization, and which many will choose not to go through.[112] Victims do not, in fact, often exercise their rights.[113] And yet, as of 2005, victims' rights had been added to 32 state constitutions.[114]

---

110 David L. Roland, "Progress in the Victims' Rights Movement: No Longer the 'Forgotten Victim,'" *Pepperdine Law Rev.* 17 (1988), 51 n. 87; Black, "Forgotten Penological Purposes," 226.

111 Black, "Forgotten Penological Purposes," 226.

112 Cunneen, "Limitations of Restorative Justice," 134–35.

113 Anne Heinz & Wayne Korstetter, "Victim Participation in Plea Bargaining: A Field Experiment," in *Plea-Bargaining*, ed. William F. MacDonald & James A. Kramer (Lexington, MA: Lexington Books, 1980), 67–77; Edwin Villmoare & Virginia U. Neto, *Victim Appearances at Sentencing Under the California Victims' Bill of Rights* (Washington, DC: U.S. Department of Justice, National Institute of Justice, 1982), 42–44; Black, "Forgotten Penological Purposes," 231.

114 Mary Achilles & Lorraine Stutzman-Amstutz, "Responding to the Needs of Victims: What Was Promised, What Was Delivered," in *Handbook of Restorative*

VR has even been proposed as an amendment to the U.S. Constitution.[115]

Dennis Sullivan & Larry Tifft (self-styled anarchists) decry victim participation in sentencing as nothing but an opportunity for victims to vent their vindictiveness.[116] They don't like *that* kind of participatory justice. They call for according victims an opportunity for "voice," but only if they say what Sullivan & Tifft want to hear. What some victims want is revenge. What the Arjays want them to say they want is repentance, forgiveness and redemption. What some victims want is compensation, but, concentrating on compensation is (they say) an "impediment to healing."[117] Using other people as means is, according to Kant, the fundamental immorality.[118] But that is what RJ does. It is clear that for RJ, victims are merely means to extraneous moral and careerist ends. It is not surprising that the major limitation on RJ aggrandizement is chronically low victim participation rates.[119] There is no reason to think that will ever change.[120]

Justice, 212–13. Stutzman-Amstutz is another Mennonite. Achilles was the appointed Victim Advocate for the Commonwealth of Pennsylvania.

115 Ibid., 213. The sponsors were Senators Dianne Feinstein (D-Cal.) and John Kyl (R-Ariz.). Both have well-earned reputations as arch-enemies of civil liberties and the rights of criminal defendants.

116 Sullivan & Tifft, *Restorative Justice*, 17.

117 Ibid., 18–19.

118 "Act so that you you use humanity, as much in your own person as in the person of any other, always at the same time as an end and never as a means." Immanuel Kant, *Groundwork for the Metaphysics of Morals*, ed. & trans. Allen W. Wood (New Haven, CT & London: Yale University Press, 2002), 46–47 (emphasis deleted); see also idem, *Critique of Practical Reason*, ed. [& trans.] Lewis White Beck (3rd ed.; New York: Macmillan Publishing Company, 1993), 138–39.

119 Williams, *Victims of Crime and Community Justice*, 69; Zernova, *Restorative Justice*, 21 (13% victim attendance at community boards), 118 n. 2 (citing four studies finding low victim attendance).

120 Incidentally, this tenet of RJ ideology refutes the claim that RJ is a return to age-old forms of reconciliation. For societies like the Plateau Tonga and the Ifugaos, either revenge or compensation, depending on the case, is not only taken for granted, it is encouraged. See also William Ian Miller, *Bloodtaking and Peacemaking: Feud, Law, and Society in Saga Iceland* (Chicago, IL: University of Chicago Press, 1990). A man who refused to exact revenge or demand compensation would be dishonored. In these societies, where honor is important, he who turns the other cheek is not

3. RJ Involves the Community, Representing Its Values, and It Reintegrates Offenders and Victims into the Community.[121]

Like the NJC advocates, the Arjays assert that one of the stakeholders is "the community," [122] and so, RJ will heal that too. But "community" is here—yet again—a feel-good meaningless word. Although RJ usually ropes in a few more participants than did the NJCs—usually just the parents of juvenile delinquents—it's a mockery to characterize the few people who attend a conference as "the community," or as the virtual representatives of a community. And yet, many Arjays do that. In an early RJ manifesto, Howard Zehr and Harry Mika used the word "community" 12 times in 5 ½ pages.[123] This is reprinted in the latest edition of Zehr's canonical bestseller *The Little Book of Restorative Justice,* which affirms Restorative Justice while denying or qualifying almost every claim ever made for it.

Social scientists have used the word community in various ways, often imprecisely. In *Keywords*, Raymond Williams identified five modern meanings of the word.[124] An earlier study identified 94 definitions of community.[125] By now there might be more. I think there are more. But, in the sense of

only despised, he can expect another slap. In our society, especially among anarchists, honor is an almost forgotten value. "I have no belief in the theory that non-resistance has, as a rule, a mollifying effect upon the aggressor. I do not wish people to turn me the other cheek when I smite them, because, in most cases, that has a bad effect upon me. I am soon used to submission and may come to think no more of the unresisting sufferer than I do of the sheep whose flesh I eat at dinner." Charles Horton Cooley, *Human Nature* (rev. ed.; New York, Schocken Books, 1964), 276 (originally 1902). "If you turn the other cheek, you will get a harder blow on it than you got on the first one." George Orwell, "Lear, Tolstoy, and the Fool," *The Collected Essays, Journalism and Letters of George Orwell*, ed. Sonia Orwell & Ian Angus (New York: Harcourt, Brace & World, 1968), 4: 298.

121 Tomasic, "Mediation as an Alternative to Adjudication," 230–32.

122 Zehr, *Little Book*, 21, 26, 84 & *passim*.

123 Howard Zehr & Harry Mika, "Fundamental Principles of Restorative Justice," in Zehr, *Little Book*, 83–89.

124 Raymond Williams, *Keywords* (new ed.; Oxford: Oxford University Press, 2015), 39.

125 G.A. Hillery, "Definitions of Community: Areas of Agreement," Rural Sociology 20 (1955), 119.

community studies, the general idea was usually to identify a locality whose population participated in a relatively dense web of social relations and whose residents identified with their community. The assumption is also that, typically, there is some continuity in time. Its highest flowering is the "organic" community.

The *locus classicus* of community is Ferdinand Tönnies, *Community and Society*. He emphasized that these are ideal types, the poles of a continuum, not a dichotomy or an evolutionary sequence, although on this point he is often misrepresented. *Gemeinschaft* (community) predominates in families, villages and some small towns. *Gesellschaft* (society) prevails in cities and states. It is an association of isolated individuals whose relations are formally voluntary, impersonal and instrumental, and entered into for advantage. It may encapsulate relatively *Gemeinschaft* formations such as guilds, congregations and certain neighborhoods. Tönnies' many criminological writings, which are untranslated and virtually unknown, did not employ the *Gemeinschaft/Gesellschaft* distinction as the master explanation of crime. He rejected the romanticization of *Gemeinschaft*[126] which persists today among communitarian academics. Impatient critical criminologists say, "time to make Tönnies and [Louis] Wirth go away!"[127]

Tönnies did quote Karl Marx and Sir Henry Maine, for whom the historical trend is from status to contract, from community to society: from kinship to locality, from custom to law, from the gift to the market, from fellowship to hierarchy, from the country to the city, and (although Tönnies does not put it this way), from anarchy to the state. They had many predecessors in drawing the distinction, arguably including Confucius, Plato, Aristotle, Cicero, Augustine, Aquinas and

---

126 Matieu Deflem, "Ferdinand Tönnies on Crime and Society: An Unexplored Contribution to Criminological Sociology," *History of the Human Sciences* 12(3) (1999): 87–116.

127 Donnermayer & DeKeseredy, *Rural Criminology*, 51. The other allusion is to Louis Wirth, "Urbanism as a Way of Life," *American J. of Sociology* 40 (1938): 1–24.

Ibn Khaldun.[128] I think Burke, de Tocqueville and Herbert Spencer also qualify. And they had many successors, such as Emile Durkheim,[129] Georges Sorel, Louis Wirth, Talcott Parsons, Robert Nisbet; and even the Situationist Raoul Vaneigem, and the political scientist Robert D. Putnam, not to mention the anthropologists.

We have seen that there are few if any organic communities in contemporary American cities. Even Tifft & Sullivan acknowledge the reality of "killed" communities.[130] But if the aforementioned grand tradition in social theory is onto something here, then Restorative Justice, if it has anything to do with community, has no future, because community has no future. Communities wither away because of the unending encroachments of secularism, capitalism and the state. And "killed" is sometimes not entirely a metaphor. As Jane Jacobs showed, American social policy after World War II deliberately destroyed many viable urban communities, most directly by "urban renewal," but also by suppressing mass transit, by financing highway construction and by financing suburban home ownership.[131] For example, Boston's South End, a mostly Italian working-class community, was destroyed in order to make way for what we now call gentrification. It had previously been, according to sociologist Herbert Gans (who lived there and studied it), an "urban village."[132] Even contemporary rural America is often not the solidary, law-abiding antithesis to urban disorganization which most sociologists assume it to be.[133]

---

128 Pitirim A. Sorokin, "Forward" to *Community and Society*, vii.

129 "Review of Ferdinand Tönnies, *Gemeinschaft und Gesellschaft*," *Emile Durkheim on Institutional Analysis*, ed. & trans. Mark Traugott (Chicago, IL & London: University of Chicago Press, 1978), 115–122.

130 "Transformative Justice and Structural Change," *Handbook of Restorative Justice*, 495.

131 Jane Jacobs, *The Death and Life of Great American Cities* (New York: The Modern Library, 1993) (originally 1961).

132 Herbert J. Gans, *The Urban Villagers: The Social Structure of an Italian Slum* (New York: Random House, 1993) (originally 1962); see also William H. Whyte, *Street Corner Society: The Social Structure of an Italian Slum* (4th ed.; Chicago, IL: University of Chicago Press, 1993).

133 Donnemeyer & DeKeseredy, *Rural Criminology*, 4–7 & *passim*.

RJ conferences can hardly be considered communities, or even representatives of communities in this or any realistic sense. Nonetheless, one RJ gambit is to define the community as "anyone who 'shows up' for a community sanctioning meeting."[134] Community is a criminological cliché: "'The community' has become the all-purpose solution to every criminal justice problem."[135] "Or, to paraphrase Jeremiah, our false prophets cry 'Community, community,' but we have no community!"[136] One fact about this "warmly persuasive word" is a constant: "unlike all other terms of social organization (*state, nation, society*, etc.) it seems never to be used unfavourably, and never to be given any positive opposing or distinguishing term."[137]

A related gambit is to keep the word but change the subject. RJ addresses community problems by redefining whatever it *does* supposedly do as addressing community problems. Never mind if only a handful of persons are concerned in the matter, and maybe not very concerned. Never mind if it's a minor matter. Now, the community is the "microcommunity"[138] of victim, offender and "the families of each, and any other members of their respective communities who may be affected, or who may be able to contribute to prevention of a recurrence [citation omitted]."[139] Not affected, just "may be affected," and not able to contribute, just maybe able to contribute. In the "Wagga Wagga" model (Australia), the conference takes place at the police station: "The 'community' is a panel of police sergeants."[140]

---

134 George Bazemore & David R. Karp, "Community Justice Sanctioning Models: Assessing Program Integrity," in *Restorative Justice: Repairing Communities*, 192. Even without an invitation?

135 David Garland, *The Culture of Control: Crime and Social Order in Contemporary Society* (Oxford: Oxford University Press, 2011), 123. Or if not "community," "family."

136 Gilligan, *Preventing Violence*, 11.

137 Williams, *Keywords*, 40.

138 Paul McCold & Benjamin Wachtel, "Community Is Not a Place: A New Look at Criminal Justice Initiatives," in *Restorative Justice: Repairing Communities through Restorative Justice*, 46. Community *is* a place or it is a myth.

139 Tony Marshall, quoted in ibid., 46.

140 Takagi & Shenk, "Critique of Restorative Justice," 156.

The "respective communities"—is this an infinite regress? Defining a community by reference to members of other, equally suppositious communities? The families of victim and offender, who will usually be strangers to one another—even if victim and offender are not—may not be neighbors, and may not share any social networks, and may not share the same values. And yet, this accidental temporary aggregate, this handful of individuals is taken to be the *vox populi*, the voice of community morality: "The role of the community in restorative justice . . . is to establish the boundaries of the community, to set the moral norms. The community provides the forum in which justice can occur."[141] What does "establish the boundaries of the community" mean? Nothing.

And so "the concept of restoring the community remains a mystery, as indeed does the identification of the relevant 'community.'"[142] How do you heal a community if you don't even know if there is one? Or what it is? And who says the community needs healing, just because somebody committed a crime there, which happens every day, everywhere? How do you heal an abstraction? Nonetheless, the cant of community persists in an evidentiary void and as an open affront to common knowledge.

In primitive societies, as I have related, individual conflicts concern the community because the disputants have ties to kin groups, and sometimes also other groups, which are implicated because these groups are responsible for the wrongs of their members. They don't need healing. They just need to resolve intergroup conflict. That's not true of a modern urban society. There, often there exist no such groups, kin-based or anything-based. Only a few crimes have community-wide ramifications, by any definition of community. Modern society is largely a society of strangers, as de Tocqueville, Tönnies, Durkheim and Cooley maintained. For most city dwellers and

---

141 John G. Perry, "Challenging the Assumptions," in *Restorative Justice: Repairing Communities*, 11.

142 Andrew Ashworth, *Sentencing and Criminal Justice* (5th ed.; Cambridge: Cambridge University Press, 2010), 94.

suburbanites, even your next door neighbors—or the tenants in the adjacent apartment—don't know you very well. They feel no responsibility for helping you solve your personal problems. In a society as alienated as ours is, why should they? They don't expect you to solve their problems either. Most Americans live in "killed neighborhoods."[143]

The criminal law has always recognized, as a stakeholder, an actor more encompassing than the criminal, the victim and others immediately involved: *the state*. In a statist society, the state is the only organized organ of the entire "community." It establishes its own boundaries, by war if necessary. Indeed, the only meaningful definition of "community" is "the population which the state governs." The community is shadowy, but the state is solid. The state expropriates many conflicts, and also monopolizes the means of their resolution.[144] It creates a civil law system for private disputes in which it has (usually) no direct interest, beyond keeping the peace and sustaining property relations. It creates a criminal law system for disputes to which it deems itself to be a party. The state claims to be hurt by any crime, even if it harms no one else. Anti-statists have always objected to this, but we at least recognize the state as a deplorable reality. Claims of harm to unidentifiable, phantom communities are meaningless. Injuries to imagined communities[145] cannot be repaired any more than can injuries to Oz, or Never-Never Land, or Middle Earth, or the Abbey of Theleme, or Walden Two, or Anarres, because they are only imaginary.

RJ does not object to this reification, since RJ advances the less credible claim that, in the words of Howard Zehr, "the problem of crime—and wrongdoing in general—is that it represents a wound in the community, a tear in the web of relationships."[146] By "wrongdoing in general" he means, of course,

---

143 Sullivan & Tifft, "Introduction," *Restorative Justice*, 6. The phrase "killed communities" is from Nils Christie, "Conflicts as Property," 12.

144 Christie, "Conflicts as Property."

145 I borrow the phrase from Benedict Anderson, *Imagined Communities: Reflections on the Origins and Spread of Nationalism* (rev. ed.; London & New York: Verso, 1991).

146 Zehr, *Little Book*, 29.

not crime, but sin. Sullivan & Tifft: "Part of the restorative process entails healing the original harm *or sin* . . ."[147] Since most sins are not crimes,[148] except in Iran and Saudi Arabia, it is against the best interests of us sinners for the distinction to be blurred. The result will usually be, not to treat crimes as sins, but to treat sins as crimes, as the Puritans did and as the mullahs do. It never occurs to Sullivan, Tifft, Zehr & Co. that *law* might represent a wound in the community, and a tear in the web of relationships.

Tifft & Sullivan, with their social science Ph.Ds, can say— this is so grotesque, they must actually believe it: "No one of us can be harmed or traumatized without all of us suffering and no one of us can prosper without all of us gaining in our common identity and well-being."[149] If they, like former President Bill Clinton, *feel our pain*, they must be in a lot of pain. But you don't understand the first thing about modern society if you don't understand that it is precisely there that an injury to one is *not* an injury to all. If it were, nobody would injure anybody. And the wealthy few, the 1%, have prospered at the expense of the majority for the last 40 years, "without all of us gaining in our common identity and well-being." They're not feeling any pain. They're feeling good. They're on a roll.

4. RJ Reduces Recidivism.[150]

There was no evidence that NJCs reduce recidivism. I've cited some of the studies. Does RJ? The Arjays often take the high ground here (a Mount is a good place from which to preach a Sermon); while vaguely claiming some success here too—as, indeed, everywhere—Howard Zehr writes: "Nevertheless, reduced recidivism is not the primary reason for operating restorative justice programs. Reduced recidivism is a byproduct,

---

147 Sullivan & Tifft, *Restorative Justice*, 164 (emphasis added).

148 Lysander Spooner, *Vices Are Not Crimes: A Vindication of Moral Liberty* (originally 1875), available at oll.thelibertyfund.org/titles/2292. Unlike Sullivan & Tifft, Spooner was an anarchist.

149 Sullivan & Tifft, "Introduction," 14.

150 Tomasic, "Mediation as an Alternative to Adjudication," 242.

but restorative justice is done first of all because it is the right thing to do."[151] The religious moralism is undisguised here. If, for adjudication, often the process is the punishment, for RJ, the process is its own reward. It is intrinsically good. It is even, some say, "a way of life"![152] Thank God for criminals! That is reminiscent of the San Francisco Community Boards whose best documented accomplishment was the personal growth of the mediators.

However, the heavens are where manna falls from, and good manna is hard to find. Governments don't fund RJ, and courts don't compel criminals to submit to its loving embrace, because that is the right thing to do. Governments are not in the right-thing-to-do business, although they have no objection if what they do, for their own reasons, happens to coincide with the right thing to do. Where governments invent or incorporate RJ programs, that is partly for public relations, to take credit for RJ's dubious utility for crime control. RJ has always depended on the state for both its funding and its referrals. The trend is for that dependence to continue and to increase.

Unlike the NJCs, RJ has apparently not claimed to be faster and cheaper than adjudication, although I may have overlooked something. It couldn't very well do that. Certainly that was no part of its original rationale. Like the NJCs, RJ is labor-intensive. It is also capital-intensive. Its facilitators and convenors are supposed to be graduates of training programs. There is no pretense this time that they are just volunteer public-spirited neighborhood people. They are paraprofessionals. They have jobs. They and their support staffs have to be paid. The adjudication, except for sentencing, is usually complete when RJ is called in. RJ can be used for pre-trial or

---

151 Zehr, *Little Book*, 16.

152 Zehr, *Little Book*, 11; see also Fred Boehrer, "The Good Samaritan or the Person in the Ditch? An Attempt to Live a Restorative Justice Lifestyle," in *Handbook of Restorative Justice*, 546–554 (a history of Emmaus House, a "Catholic Worker house" in Albany, New York, inspired by the Catholic anarchist Dorothy Day). I live in Albany. I know about Emmaus House. It offers short-term room and board for a few homeless people. What this has to do with RJ, I have no idea.

pre-sentencing diversion;[153] that is its main use in Europe.[154] RJ diversion programs are apparently less common here.

With noticeable reluctance, the Arjays are making claims that RJ reduces recidivism (reoffending). That's because they know which side their bread is buttered on. They need bread in order to put on their circuses. An early study by Mark S. Umbreit, whose devotion to RJ is fanatical, found that RJ reduced recidivism, but the difference was not statistically significant.[155] Arjays made more of this claim in the early days when there was little evidence. But now, as another RJ ideologue ruefully remarks: "They claimed, for example, that restorative justice would dramatically cut reoffending rates. When it began to be apparent that it did not, it was easy for politicians, police officers and others juggling tight budgets to disregard its other possible benefits."[156] Actually, often they did discern "other possible benefits"—to themselves. Discernment is often most acute when motivated by self-interest.

One major "meta-study"—a study of studies—on the issue of recidivism was published in 2005. The article makes the point that even studies asserting statistically significant

---

153 Shapland, Robinson & Sorsby, *Restorative Justice in Practice*, 7; Zehr, *The Little Book*, 66–67.

154 Pelikan & Trenczek, "Victim Offender Mediation and Restorative Justice," 82.

155 Mark S. Umbreit, "Restorative Justice Through Victim-Offender Mediation: A Multi-Site Assessment," *Western Criminology Rev.* 1(1) (June 1998) (unpaginated), available online at http://www.westerncriminology.org/documents/WCR/v01n1/Umbreit/umbreit.html. This is the same guy whose first RJ book had a chapter on "Biblical Justice." If you consider the Old Testament to be the Bible, as Jews do, or as part of the Bible, as Christians do, you do *not* want Biblical justice. The New Testament only looks better by comparison. In another of his innumerable RJ articles, Umbreit mentions the statistics from his own study—but not the fact that the difference in recidivism rates was not statistically significant. George Bazemore & Marc Umbreit, "A Comparison of Four Restorative Conferencing Models by the Office of Juvenile Justice and Delinquency Prevention," in *Restorative Justice: Repairing Communities*, 71. I'm pretty sure that Umbreit is another Mennonite, but I haven't found the smoking gun, since Mennonites are nonviolent. They leave violence to the police, and preserve their personal purity. Some positive evaluations of RJ are blatantly worthless. One 1994 study found that jurisdictions with RJ have slightly lower recidivism rates than jurisdictions which do not. Strickland, *Restorative Justice,* 26. This is known as the Ecological Fallacy, even aside from the issue of statistical significance.

156 Hoyle, "The Case for Restorative Justice," 94.

reductions in recidivism "can be misleading, especially when sample size is small."[157] They are always small: RJ is a boutique version of criminal justice. There are further pertinent and interesting methodological reservations, which I will mostly pass over.

To study recidivism, you have to follow up on the offender. Often, these studies are conducted by the RJ paraprofessionals themselves, who are not disinterested, who lack methodological sophistication and who are inclined to follow up on offenders only as long as it takes to document a happy ending. A few studies have carried on further. The authors identified 39 studies, mostly from the United States, whose methodology was, in their view, up to professional standards.[158] The average interval before a follow-up study was 17.7 months.[159] That's not very long. Of almost all reoffending studies it may be said, as was said of one of them, "the evaluation did not include contacting respondents again a considerable time into the future."[160]

The meta-study concluded:

> 1. RJ "interventions" resulted in small, but statistically significant reductions in recidivism in these minor cases of white male juvenile delinquency.

> 2. "There is evidence that court-ordered RJ programs have no effect on recidivism."

---

157 James Bonta, Rececca Jesseman, Tanya Rugge & Robert Cormier, "Restorative Justice and Recidivism: Promises Made, Promises Kept?" in *Handbook of Restorative Justice*, 110.

158 Ibid., 113.

159 Ibid., 114. The authors report that "most of the offenders in the restorative justice programs were low-risk, male, Caucasian youth. Very few programs targeted serious cases such as violent offenders or those who committed crimes against the person." For some reason, I am not surprised that these whiteboys "displayed very high rates of satisfaction with restorative justice." Ibid.

160 Shapland, Robinson & Sorsby, *Restorative Justice in Practice*, 166. Here is an astounding admission from a seven-year study of three English programs: "In talking about reducing or ceasing offending, it is also important to recognise that this is only a relevant question if the perpetrator has a previous history of offending." Ibid., 176. What! Only academics are interested in recidivism *per se*. Everybody else wants to know if a criminal will offend, whether or not he has offended before.

3. RJ is more effective with low-risk offenders, but not very effective with high-risk offenders. (In other words: offenders who were less likely to reoffend, reoffended less often than offenders who were more likely to reoffend. That's brilliant. Just like the conventional court system.[161])

The authors also report that RJ appears to be becoming more effective (but that is merely an impression as of 2005). Even if that's true, the improvement is offset by the fact that court-ordered RJ programs have no effect on recidivism. Virtually all RJ programs in the United States, and probably elsewhere (Australia, New Zealand, Britain) are by now court-annexed. The best evidence available indicates that these programs "have no effect on recidivism."

The main reason why RJ cannot do very much to reduce recidivism is that RJ cannot do very much of anything, for the same reason the NJCs could not. The caseloads are too small. Even high rates of success, however defined, could not have much effect on crime rates. RJ for juvenile offenders has been in place in New South Wales (where it is administered by the police) since the 1990s. It claims "modest benefits in reduction of re-offending compared to court." But only "between 2 and 4 percent of police interventions involving young people result in referral to a youth justice conference."[162]

The most comprehensive study in Europe of RJ effectiveness, especially with respect to recidivism, was published in April 2010. It concluded that evaluations of RJ effectiveness, especially as to recidivism, are "weak," often methodologically unsound, "and largely relate impressions rather than statistical proof."[163]

As with the NJCs, measurements of success are easy to rig. Cases where offenders decline RJ—if they have a choice—are

---

161 Bonta *et al.*, "Restorative Justice and Recidivism," 117.

162 Chris Cunneen, "The Limits of Restorative Justice," in *Debating Restorative Justice*, 184.

163 *Restorative Justice and Crime Prevention: Presenting a Theoretical Exploration, an Empirical Analysis and the Policy Perspective* (April 2010), 173.

not scored as failures. Cases where victims decline to participate in the charade (these are much more frequent) are not scored as failures. Cases where offenders reoffend, but not within the relatively short periods in which they are followed up on, are not scored as failures. Sample sizes are small and there is usually not a control group by which to determine if offenders would not have reoffended anyway if they went through the conventional court system.[164] There are deeply moving anecdotes, like the story of the Prodigal Son. But that was not even an anecdote: it was a parable.

Possibly I am being unfair to the Arjays. Some conflicts and disputes—according to Richard Abel, most conflicts and disputes—eventuate, not in settlements or resolutions, but, possibly after a respite, in more conflicts and disputes.[165] Serious longitudinal studies of adjudication or various other forms of ADR in modern societies might also find many failures in the long term. But *tu quoque* is not a justification.

---

[164] Zernova, *Restorative Justice*, 32.

[165] Richard Abel, "A Comparative Theory of Dispute Institutions in Society," *Law & Society Rev.* (1983), 228.

9. "Reintigrative Shaming"

Unlike the NJCs, where theory preceded practice, for Restorative Justice, practice preceded theory. NJC accumulated various ad hoc rationales as time went by. But there is a theory, invented by an author who was then unacquainted with RJ, which some Arjays have pressed into service: "reintegrative shaming." In a book published in 1989,[1] Australian criminologist John Braithwaite argued that "the theory of reintegrative shaming explains compliance with the law by the moralizing qualities of social control rather than by its repressive qualities." The inner cop replaces the outer cop. Except he never does. Where there was one cop, now there are two.

Everywhere, Braithwaite claims, there is an overwhelming moral consensus in favor of the criminal law. I doubt it. He thinks that consensus is a (morally) good thing too. He further asserts—and this is certainly false—that most people know most of what the law forbids. No lawyer or judge knows what the law forbids. There are, for example, over 175,000 pages in the Code of Federal Regulations, which is not even a complete statement of Federal regulations. Recently, a court held that the U.S. Department of Health and Human Services did not even understand its own regulations.[2] If people

---

[1] John Braithwaite, *Crime, Shame and Reintegration* (previously cited). I will not be providing specific page citations. The book, though short, is repetitious. You don't have to look very long to find anything.

[2] *Caring Hearts Personal Services, Inc. v. Burwell*, No. 14–3243 (10th Cir., May 31, 2016).

knew more about the law, they would respect it even less than they do.[3]

Braithwaite was unaware of RJ in 1989, but they were made for each other. By 2002 he was a major RJ theorist.[4] Reintegrative shaming is the closest thing to a theory which RJ has. Not everybody is happy about that. Howard Zehr writes:

> The topic is highly controversial, however, and the best research [which is not cited] suggests that shame is indeed a factor in both victimization and offending, but it has to be handled very carefully. In most situations, the focus needs to be on managing or transforming shame rather than imposing it.[5]

Is he saying that shaming is part of the problem, not part of the solution? If he is, he got that part right.

Repression is never defined. It apparently approximates the punitive approach deplored by RJs. It is ineffective (Braithwaite argues) to control crime. Instead of bringing the offender back into the community, it may drive him into criminal subcultures which are largely outside the moral consensus. (But, . . . if everybody believes in the morality of law, how can there be criminal subcultures?) Instead of being punished in the usual fashion, the criminal must be made to feel *shame*, express contrition and be reconciled to the community: "A shaming ceremony followed later by a forgiveness and repentance ceremony more potently builds commitment to the law than one-sided moralizing." Braithwaite identifies few such ceremonies, but RJ was already performing such ceremonies. Indeed, nobody else does that, not since the 17th century in Puritan Massachusetts.

If criminals believe so staunchly in the criminal law, they should not need a ceremony to remind them to be ashamed of

---

3 *E.g.*, Dick Hyman, *The Trenton Pickle Ordinance and Other Bonehead Legislation* (Baltimore, MD: Penguin Books, 1984) (originally 1976).

4 John Braithwaite, *Restorative Justice and Responsible Regulation* (Oxford: Oxford University Press, 2002).

5 Zehr, *Little Book of Restorative Justice*, 101 n. 3. What social engineers have the expertise to do that?

themselves. The criminal justice process, which is a sequence of degradation ceremonies[6] beginning with arrest, will provide painful reminders. Braithwaite admits this. But his way of shaming is different, and better:

> The distinction is between shaming that leads to stigmatization—to outcasting, to confirmation of a deviant master status—versus shaming that is reintegrative, that shames while maintaining bonds of respect or love, that sharply terminates disapproval with forgiveness, instead of amplifying social deviance by progressively casting the deviant out. Reintegrative shaming controls crime; stigmatization pushes offenders toward criminal subcultures.[7]

But what if, as is not rare, the offender is *already* a member of a criminal subculture? What if there *are no* "bonds of respect or love"? Bonds with whom? The victim? Braithwaite isn't interested in victims. It is truly obscene to use the word "love" in this context. It has been clear at least since the 1950s "that there is a [juvenile] delinquent subculture, and that it is a normal, integral and deeply-rooted feature of the American city."[8] Implicitly, Braithwaite—conservative methodological individualist that he is—assumes that the cause of youth crime, and maybe all street crime, is individual maladjustment. To show that he would need some psychogenic theory of crime which he does not articulate.

Thus far this is not a "theory," and nor is it merely a hypothesis or even merely a policy proposal. It doesn't explain anything, even if (as Braithwaite claims) it may not be *inconsistent* with the criminological research available in 1989. That's not saying much. He needs some sociological underpinning. It's the usual dumbed-down Durkheim: "Individuals are more susceptible to shaming when they are enmeshed in

---

[6] Harold Garfinkel, "Conditions of Successful Degradation Ceremonies," *American J. of Sociology* 61(5) (March 1956): 420–424. One of Garfinkel's examples is the criminal trial.

[7] Braithwaite, *Crime, Shame and Reintegration* (previously cited).

[8] Albert K. Cohen, *Delinquent Boys: The Culture of the Gang* (New York, The Free Press & London: Collier-Macmillan Limited, 1955), 18.

multiple relationships of interdependency; societies shame more effectively when they are communitarian." In other words, multiplex relationships, cross-cutting ties and roots in a stable community—the usual. Braithwaite is even more evasive about what a community is than were his future allies, the Arjays. He appears to consider Japan—the poster child for reintegrative shaming—to be a community. He lifted that from Ruth Benedict's "shame culture" notion.[9] The word he should have learned from her was just "culture." Subcultures are nested in cultures.

Braithwaite proposes a "family model of the criminal process: reintegrative shaming." The family model of society is fascism. The criminal justice process is nothing like a family, not even a dysfunctional family. Japan, about which Braithwaite knows very little, is not a family. American cities, and their neighborhoods, even the more homogeneous ones, are nothing like families. Even some of their actual families are nothing like families on the traditional model. So, like some Arjays, Braithwaite speaks of "communities *of interest*"—this one goes all the way back to Richard Danzig's powwow among the juvenile loiterer, the nervous store owner and anybody else he could think of. If reintegrative shaming works—just as for RJ—it only works in exceptional circumstances. It's not a new paradigm for criminal justice. It's another peripheral state-controlled practice. If more widely operationalized, it would have a negligible effect on crime rates. Some RJ processes do operationalize the theory, more or less. We have seen that the results are unimpressive.

The "family model" is appropriate—if even then—to only one institution: the family itself. And the modern nuclear family has many cogent critics, including feminists, anarchists, and—until they got the right to marry each other—homosexuals.

RJ processes, such victim-offender conferences, are mostly futile, but mostly harmless—although it bears remembering that in one study, 25% of the victims felt *worse*

---

[9] Ruth Benedict, *The Crysanthemum and the Sword: Patterns of Japanese Culture* (Cleveland, OH: Meridian Books, 1967).

afterwards. Reintegrative shaming is potentially dangerous, as even Braithwaite admits: "However, for all types of crime, shaming runs the risk of counterproductivity when it shades into stigmatization." Howard Zehr worried about this. The social engineering for shaming to be reliably reintegrative rather than stigmatizing does not exist and it never will. In Japan, they have a long history of shaming. It can be reintegrative. But Japanese who have been shamed may commit suicide.

Braithwaite has next to nothing to say about how to institutionalize reintegrative shaming in an (as he sees it) extremely individualistic society such as the United States. He can only express hope that this country is (as he thought it might be) moving slowly in a communitarian direction. It wasn't. He wrote this book while Ronald Reagan was President! And the United States is still not, in any sense of the word, communitarian. That would require a social revolution. A social revolution would require that many people reject the supposed moral consensus in support of the law. A revolution is always something immoral.[10]

If the word "community" is vague to the point of often being meaningless, "communitarian" is worse. It appears, often more than once, on 28 of Braithwaite's 186 pages. His definition of "communitarianism":

> (1) densely intermeshed dependency, where the interdependency is characterized by (2) mutual obligation and trust, and (3) are interpreted as a matter of group loyalty rather than individual convenience. Communitarianism is therefore the antithesis of individualism.

This would include youth gangs and the Mafia.[11] Another word for the antithesis of individualism is "authoritarianism." Braithwaite isn't hip to the distinction between contraries and

---

10 Stirner, *The Ego and Its Own*, 53.

11 Francis A.J. Ianni with Elizabeth Reuss-Ianni, *A Family Business: Kinship and Social Control in Organized Crime* (New York: Russell Sage Foundation, 1972), 84, 155 & *passim*.

contradictories. He can't even imagine that there is any value in personal liberty.

If any modern industrial country approximates communitarianism, the author does not say so. Japan doesn't. Even Singapore doesn't. Braithwaite's "densely intermeshed interdependency" characterizes any society with a complex division of labor: this is old hat: this is Durkheim's organic solidarity and Tőnnies' *Gesellschaft*. His "mutual obligation and trust" does not characterize any state society. His "group loyalty" nostrum reads as a vulgarization of the Greek, Roman and colonial American ideologies of public virtue, which, in modern societies, characterizes only the official ideologies of fascist states. No admittedly fascist state now exists, although North Korea and possibly Singapore are good for "group loyalty." Even Braithwaite admits that he would not want to live in Japan. It never occurs to him that some of these three characteristics may be in tension with some of the others. That would explain why they are never all found together. It would explain why, in other words, communitarian societies are nonexistent. Modern state societies cannot be communitarian. Their legal systems cannot be communitarian.

Historically, *Gemeinschaft* gave rise to *Gesellschaft*, but *Gesellschaft* does not give rise to *Gemeinschaft*. Tőnnies, a socialist, believed that socialism was the final expression of *Gesellschaft* but that it would give rise to a modern version of *Gemeinschaft*. Marx, a communist, believed the same thing: state socialism (a necessary stage) would soon wither away. The government of men would be replaced by the administration of things; and, in higher-stage communism, there would be no state, only a free association of producers, in which the principle is from each according to his abilities and to each according to his needs. Braithwaite & Zehr and the Arjays don't go there.

Braithwaite understands that social control is almost completely based on informal sanctioning. I often make this point. But the criminal justice system, by definition, cannot engage in informal sanctioning. It is, by definition, formal. My thesis throughout this monograph is that formal state justice destroys primitive, anarchist justice. Supporters of the NJCs back in the day, and supporters of RJ today, have tried and failed to squirm out of this dilemma. In his tenure book, Braithwaite has not even tried.

Braithwaite occasionally nods at primitive societies, but he may know even less about them than the early Arjays did. Consider my examples of primitive societies. Ifugao disputing is the *antithesis* of reintegrative shaming. Its purpose is to achieve reconciliation, or at least forbearance, *without* shaming anybody. Shaming would defeat the purpose. The Ifugaos are proud individualists. Nobody apologizes for anything. Among the Plateau Tonga, likewise, shaming plays no role.

The Kpelle "moot" is the only example which is even superficially similar to reintegrative shaming. It involves a group process or ceremony, culminating in a public, pro forma apology by the wrongdoer. What follows is not absolution, but rather a beer party on the defendant's dime. Nobody has to be reintegrated because nobody was *de*-integrated in the first place. There was merely a minor dispute. When, in a primitive society, an intolerable person is finally de-integrated—outlawed—that is irreversible. Then he is dead meat.

One of Braithwaite's many shortcomings is that he does not, as he admits, really understand the difference, in practice, between guilt and shame. In this respect he resembles the Puritans, perhaps not as they really were, but as they are portrayed in *The Scarlet Letter*. For him, shaming just *is* making someone feel guilty. No doubt shame and guilt are often both involved in particular cases. That may be a reason to avoid both of them.

Although the subject is too large to develop here, *guilt* corresponds to a felt private sense of *sin*, whereas *shame* corresponds to a felt sense of public dishonor.[12] Dishonor can result, not only from what you do, but from what someone does to you, where that is publicly known. Absolution from sin results from contrition and forgiveness. Shame is dispelled by erasing

---
12 Taylor, *Community, Anarchy and Liberty*, 84.

the dishonor by revenge or by—*if* accepted—an equivalent, by compensation. Guilt and shame, although they can be confused by the confused, are fundamentally different.

The difference between guilt cultures (like ours) and shame cultures (such as traditional Japan, Homeric Greece, other Mediterranean societies and Muslim societies) has been discussed by various scholars, and Braithwaite is slightly acquainted with the literature,[13] although he has trouble understanding it. Very likely, the distinction is also lost on most other Australians, Americans and Westerners. In shaking off our aristocracies, we also shook off their values, instead of generalizing them. Nietzsche deplored this. So do I. Raoul Vaneigem, in a wonderful phrase, called for "masters without slaves,"[14] but the masses are a conglomeration of slaves, either with, or—more or less—without masters. Their servitude is voluntary.[15] Where no master is available, people enslave themselves. They have, as Max Stirner reproached them, *wheels in their heads*.[16]

Shame culture is not quite extinct in Western societies. But there, the sense of honor is either a not very common personal value, or else it's a value for what Braithwaite calls criminal subcultures (of which he disapproves).[17] It's not a value for college professors. It's not a value for leftists. It's not a value for feminists. It's not a value for most radicals. It's not even a value

---

13 *E.g.*, Ruth Benedict, *The Crysanthemum and the Sword: Patterns of Japanese Culture* (Boston, MA: Houghton Mifflin, 1946); *Honour and Shame: The Values of Mediterranean Society*, ed. J.G. Peristiany (Chicago, IL: Universityof Chicago Press, 1966).

14 Raoul Vaneigem, *The Revolution of Everyday Life*, trans. Donald Nicolson-Smith (Oakland, CA: PM Press, 2012), ch. 21.

15 Étienne de la Boétie, *The Politics of Obedience: The Discourse of Voluntary Servitude* (Auburn, AL: Mises Institute, 2015).

16 Stirner, *The Ego and Its Own*, 43. Is it inconsistent for an amoral egoist to talk like this? Not at all. We are not precluded from having values or preferring that more people shared them. We want a world of masters without slaves. We want a world which is rational without being regulated. The fewer the dupes of morality and ideology, the better for all concerned. Egoists prefer to deal with other egoists. Bob Black, "Anarchism and Human Rights" (2016), available online at www.academia.edu.

17 Anderson, *Code of the Street*.

for anarchists who suppose that they are avant garde. In fact, among the anarchists, I've found less of a sense of honor, and less of a sense of solidarity, than among any kind of people I have ever associated with. There is more honor on elementary school playgrounds. And on ghetto streets. The notion that an injury to one is an injury to all elicits only laughter in the Bay Area anarchist scene. That is something to put on the masthead of an IWW newspaper, not to put into practice.

The main problem with reintegrative shaming is that—as a matter of social psychology—it is, as a theory of crime-control policy, totally wrong. Shaming is not the main solution for violent street crime. Shaming is the main cause of violent street crime.

At least, it's the main cause of the violent crimes which inspire so much fear. James Gilligan, a psychiatrist who worked for many years with the most violent criminals in Massachusetts prisons, has written about this. Violent criminals are people (mostly men) who have been shamed:

> the basic psychological motive, or cause, of violent behavior is to ward off or eliminate the feeling of shame or humiliation—a feeling that is painful, and that can be intolerable and overwhelming—and replace it with its opposite, a feeling of pride.[18]

One implication, which is consistent with such as there is of anarchist criminology, is that "punishment is the most violent stimulus to violent behavior that we have discovered. . . . Punishment does not prevent crime, it causes it."[19] Kropotkin and Berkman would have agreed. Where respect is not spontaneously forthcoming, the direct and certain way to gain

---

18 Gilligan, *Preventing Violence*, 29. The argument is more fully worked out in James Gilligan, *Violence: Reflections on Our Deadliest Epidemic* (London & Philadelphia, PA: Jessica Kingsley Publishers, 2000) (originally 1996).

19 Ibid., 18 (emphasis omitted). Why did Cain slay Abel? Because (Genesis 4:5 (KJV)) the "Lord had *respect* unto Abel and his offering: But unto Abel . . . he had not *respect*." "And Cain was very wroth, and his countenance fell." Cain slew Abel because "God 'dis'd' Cain. Or rather, Cain was 'dis'd' because of Abel—and he acted out his anger over this insult in exactly the same way as the murderers with whom I was working." Gilligan, *Preventing Violence,* 31. Jehovah is a piss-poor social psychologist.

respect is by instilling fear.[20] This is also how police, who are despised by everybody, coerce respect.

Who's right, Braithwaite or Gilligan? Surely much more Gilligan than Braithwaite. More important, why should either opinion be institutionalized by the state? Attempts to base policy on policy science, as with the NJCs, are usually fiascos. Because these theories are irrelevant unless they are, as they both obviously are, policy prescriptions. Braithwaite & Co. have written advice books for rulers, like the medieval and Renaissance books which were often titled *A Mirror for Princes*. Erasmus wrote one, under another title. Machiavelli's *The Prince* is another example, also under another title, although not a typical example. The state has usually ignored the advice of criminologists, even on the rare occasions when it was good advice. May that continue.

---

20 Gilligan, *Preventing Violence,* 53.

10. The Anarchist Academics: A Sorry Story

THE ANARCHIST ACADEMICS are by now almost as welcome in academia as the Marxist academics are,[1] and for the same reason. They're harmless, but they add a touch of the picturesque. Their inclusion is all the easier because they are almost indistinguishable from the Marxists, who by now have tenure. And what did *Marx* think of criminologists?

> A philosopher produces ideas, a poet poems, a professor compendia, and so on. A criminal produces crimes. If we look a little closer at the connection between this latter branch of production and society as a whole, we shall rid ourselves of many prejudices. The criminal produces not only crimes but also criminal law, *and with this also the professor who gives lectures on criminal law and in addition to this the inevitable compendium in which this same professor throws his lectures into the general market as "commodities."*[2]

What, then, does an anarchist criminologist espouse? Not anarchy! He espouses "restorative justice."

I've already scorned Larry Tifft and Dennis Sullivan, who

---

[1] Although—in 2004—David Graeber complained: "In the United States there are thousands of academic Marxists of one sort or another, but hardly a dozen scholars willing openly to call themselves anarchists." *Fragments of an Anarchist Anthropology*, 2. Now there are more—although there was one less when Yale fired Graeber, recently deceased.

[2] Karl Marx, *Theories of Surplus Value,* trans. Emile Burns, ed. S. Ryazanskaya (Moscow: Foreign Languages Publishing House, 1963), 1: 387–88 (emphasis added).

are apparently the first avowed anarchist criminologists. They are bleeding-heart radicals with a conventional leftist critique of law and the state as tools of the powerful—only their version is more than usually sentimental and mystical. Despite their opportunity to be more up-to-date and well-informed than the classical anarchists, these two, in their 1980 book, added nothing to the stale old leftist critique except a few hippie grace notes. I thought they would drop out of the academy. Given their ideology, they could no more make research contributions to criminology (necessary for tenure) than a creation scientist could make research contributions to biology (necessary for tenure).

Instead, they found a way to have it both ways: Restorative Justice. A review comparing their 1980 and 2001 books recognized that the second book is to some degree an attempt to redress the shortcomings of the first, but "it is still the case that specific details as to how alternative systems would deal with acts such as theft, assault, rape, or murder are sorely lacking here."[3]

A 1998 article by one Jeff Ferrell, now Professor of Sociology at Texas Christian University—which has been reprinted in at least five anthologies which I have no intention of looking at—is just an epitome of Tifft & Sullivan (1980), adding nothing except a few post-modernist flourishes.[4] It gets anthologized to show how hip the publishers are. Then it's back to business, pimping for the state. But by then, Tifft & Sullivan had discovered Restorative Justice. Today, these anarchists are among the foremost expositors and advocates of RJ. Ferrell has apparently not dabbled in Restorative Justice. It's not edgy enough.

I've come across several brief online articles linking anarchism to RJ which show no critical understanding of either.[5] I

---

3 Randall Amster, "Breaking the Law: Anti-Authoritarian Visions of Crime and Justice," *New Formulation* 2(2) (Winter–Spring 2004) (unpaginated), available at http://newformulation.org/4Amster.htm.

4 Jeff Ferrell, "Against the Law: Anarchist Criminology," available online at www.socialanarchism.org.

5 Coy McKinney, "An Anarchist Theory of Criminal Justice," May 2012, available at www.theanarchistlibrary.org, is based entirely on one article and one book about

came across another one by Brian Gumm—yet another guy whose name is not yet a household word in anarchist households—"The Anarchist Genius of Restorative Justice?" He is a "lay theologian," a former student of Howard Zehr, and, like Zehr, a Mennonite.[6] If Howard Zehr is an anarchist, which he has never claimed, he has fooled everybody, including himself, for forty years. The only thing anarchism and Restorative Justice have in common is that they are currently fashionable in small ideologically grounded subcultures. For both, their vogue may be waning.

Throughout my relatively long life, there have been fads and fashions. That time includes my several involvements with academia. My impression is that the pace is increasingly speeded up, and the turnover is faster (is this "future shock"?). The mini-skirt fashion of the 1960s, despite the bitter resistance of gay fashion designers, stubbornly persisted for longer than did the NJC fad of the 1980s. Of course there still exists the occasional NJC, just as one occasionally sees a *jeune fille* in a mini-skirt. More often, actually.

RJ may still be expanding, here and around the world. It

RJ. The book is—what else?—Howard Zehr, *The Little Book of Restorative Justice* (2002 edition, published in Intercourse, PA). Megan Petrucelli, "Beyond Absolutes: Justice for All," available at http://anarchiststudies.org/2016/01/27/beyond-absolutes-justice-for-all-by-megan-petrucelli, after espousing anarchism in its first paragraph, goes off on a long autobiographical soliloquy about the author's victimizations, and concludes with a brief, idealized summary of RJ ideology. For someone who is beyond absolutes, she is absolutely sold on RJ. Duane Ruth-Heffelbower, "Anarchist Criminology: A New Way to Understand a Set of Proven Practices" (2011), available at http://ruth-heffelbower.us/docs/Anarchist_Criminology.pdf, does not understand that RJ is not a proven practice, as we have seen. And it is difficult to see how state-coerced practices are compatible with anarchism. These writers don't know enough about RJ *or* anarchism to notice these difficulties. Ruth-Heffelbower is an attorney and a professional mediator and arbitrator. He also has a Masters in Divinity degree from—what else?—a Mennonite seminary. He is the author of *After We're Gone: A Christian Perspective on Estate Planning for Families That Include a Dependent Member with a Disability* (3rd ed.; Goshen, IN: Mennonite Publishing Network, 2011). It's a good thing I'm not paranoid, or I might believe in an RJ Mennonite conspiracy. Peter Gelderloos is the only anarchist I know of who has heard of Restorative Justice. He doesn't like it. But he is a criminal, not a criminologist. *How Nonviolencve Protects the State* (Cambridge, MA: South End Press, 2007), 157 n. 3.

6 July 10, 2013. Available at restorativetheology.blogspot.com/2013/the-anarchist-genius-of-restorative/html.

may never go away, as the NJCs (however labeled) will never go away, because RJ has been institutionalized in court systems, universities, consulting firms, NGOs, and in demi-academic journals like the *Dispute Resolution Magazine* (published, I repeat, by the American Bar Association) and the *International Journal of Dispute Resolution*. And also in court-annexed reconciliation processes, benevolently operated by state-paid paraprofessionals. There are many conferences. There are many training programs for practitioners in many countries, and at least one graduate degree program. There are grants. All this replicates, and indeed outdoes, the NJC history.

And yet, for the anarcho-liberals Tifft & Sullivan, RJ will always be "at its core a form of insurgency and subversive in nature."[7] Tifft & Sullivan still pretend to be outsiders. I don't doubt their commitment and sincerity. But it's not unusual to find in the same person a pure heart and an empty head. Tifft & Sullivan are obviously *not* outsiders. Outsiders would not have been invited to edit the *Handbook of Restorative Justice*. The less than dynamic duo would be the Prodigal Sons of academia, except that they have never been prodigal. They didn't have to go home again. They never left. They move around a lot, but they never lack for academic appointments.

Not only Tifft & Sullivan, but lots of other Arjays of the writing kind, have repeated, long after it became monotonous, that RJ is really great: it's the conquering new "paradigm." (Poor Thomas Kuhn!) It's just that we have to expand RJ—somehow—to tackle the structural sources, the economic and social sources of interpersonal crime.[8] Never repudiate RJ:

---

7 Sullivan & Tifft, "Introduction: The Healing Dimension of Restorative Justice," 2.

8 *E.g.*, David G. Gil, "Toward a 'Radical' Paradigm of Restorative Justice," *Handbook of Restorative Justice*, 499–511—who has no idea how to do that. Nobody does. Five more citations to the "paradigm shift" claim appear in Anne-Marie McAlinden, "Are There Limits to Restorative Justice?" *Handbook of Restorative Justice*, 306. "Buddy, can youse paradigm?" Bob Black, "Let Us Prey!" *The Abolition of Work and Other Essays* (Port Townsend, WA: Loompanics Unlimited, [1986]); idem, "Afterthoughts on the Abolition of Work," *Instead of Work* (Berkeley, CA: LBC Press, 2015), 151. *Cf.* Thomas S. Kuhn, *The Structure of Scientific Revolutions* (2nd ed., enl.; Chicago, IL: University of Chicago Press, 1970). No academic text is complete which fails to cite this book. I would be remiss, had I not done so.

always expand it. But that would mean, not resolving individual conflicts, but rather *fomenting* social conflicts.

There are no individualized answers to what used to be called the Social Question. "A criminology which remains fixed at the level of individualism," writes John Braithwaite, "is the criminology of a bygone era."[9] *Any* criminology is fixed at the level of individualism, and fails to fix anything. Restorative Justice is "fixed at the level of individualism" in the same way that Protestantism (its thinly disguised sponsor) is fixed there. Here, as usual, ideologies of individualism are the enemies of individuation, and the enemies of the individual.

For Arjays, and not just the Mennonites, social conflict is bad! Violence is especially bad! (except when it is state violence to implement Restorative Justice). Sullivan & Tifft like to invoke Kropotkin, but Kropotkin was unequivocally a class-struggle revolutionary anarchist. They have written approvingly of workplace arrangements, with "restorative structures and practices," under which workers are treated a little better than usual, their ideas are listened to, they are allowed a measure of self-managed servitude, and they receive a stable income. Never mind that these enlightened businesses don't exist. These pacifists of course commend a program for worker pacification—another of their lion-and-lamb scenarios: "When this level of well-being exists in a workplace, feelings of envy and resentment toward [higher-paid] co-workers *and coordinators* [bosses] are significantly reduced. People feel restored."[10] And work harder! They're suckers. Or rather, they would-be suckers, if they existed. This never happens.

"Coordinators" is a euphemism for *bosses*. The class-collaboration ideology which Tifft & Sullivan witlessly endorse is nothing less (well, maybe even less) than the old "Progressive human resource management (HRM)" perspective in

---

9 Braithwaite, *Crime, Shame and Reintegrative Shaming,* 148.

10 Dennis Sullivan & Larry Tifft, "What Are the Implications of Restorative Justice for Society and Our Lives?" in *Critical Issues in Restorative Justice*, 398–99 (emphasis added).

industrial relations studies, which is almost forgotten today.[11] During their many tranquil years in the academy, the American workplace has become a harsher place of lower real income, longer hours and more dangerous conditions over which workers, whose levels of unionization have fallen sharply, have less influence than ever.[12] And yet Tifft & Sullivan intuit an "increased sensitivity" of bosses to the personal needs of workers![13] How many bosses do they know? It's obvious that in all their lives, neither of these guys has ever had a real job.

Anarchists should actively combat Restorative influences everywhere. We want a new world. We don't want to "restore" anything. Let's be lions, not lambs.

The expansion and entrenchment of RJ are directly proportionate to its institutionalization by the state. If some of the earliest RJ programs maintained some autonomy from the state—I haven't come across any examples—they are all now nothing but minor, auxiliary parts of the criminal justice system. They are on as long or as short a leash as courts, prosecutors and police allow them under the local arrangements. The solution has, as usual, become part of the problem. By its voluntarist and humanist pretenses, RJ in a small way legitimates the criminal justice system, and maybe it opiates a few people, as religion sometimes does.

It may be that Restorative Justice is becoming passé. An imposing *Handbook of Criminological Theory* published in 2016 does not mention it.[14]

The trouble with criminal justice reforms is that *nothing ever goes away*. Penitentiaries (the very name—evoking "penitence"—reveals an affinity with RJ), insane asylums, probation, parole, pre-trial diversion, compulsory schooling,

---

11 John Godard, *Industrial Relations: The Economy and Society* (Toronto, Canada: McGraw-Hill Ryerson Ltd., 1994), 146–152, 157; Black, "Afterthoughts on the Abolition of Work," 204–205.

12 Black, "Afterthoughts on the Abolition of Work," 209–215, 255–267 & *passim*.

13 Tifft & Sullivan, *Restorative Justice*, 184–85.

14 *The Handbook of Criminological Theory*, ed. Alex R. Piquero (Chichester, Sussex, UK: Wiley Blackwell, 2016).

indeterminate sentencing, determinate sentencing, juvenile courts, small claims courts, drug courts, community justice centers, community policing, RJ, reintegrative shaming—we still have all of them somewhere, and we have most of them everywhere. Their coexistence is proof that the system is incoherent. But coherence is not a requirement for social control. In Germany, the Nazi Party, the Gestapo, the S.S., military courts, state police, local police and local courts had overlapping, often vaguely defined jurisdictions. There were jails, prisons, mental hospitals, labor camps and concentration camps operated by various authorities—something for everybody who fell afoul of a Kafkaesque system: "The confusion of powers liberated policy-makers from the constraints of morality and law."[15] Redundancy is functional for systems.

Anarchist criminologists can probably do little to de-legitimate the state. But they can do at least as much as I've done here. Instead, they legitimate the state by indirection, by pretending that there isn't always an iron fist inside the velvet glove. Unlike me, they get paid to write books and articles. They are writing the wrong books and articles.

Aside from Ferrell's 1998 article in *Social Anarchism*, the anarcho-criminologists have hitherto not, to my knowledge, addressed their fellow anarchists. And Ferrell said nothing about RJ, with which by then he must have been familiar. RJ programs originated even before the NJCs did, and they have long outlived them, regrettably. But, like the NJCs, they have never involved large numbers of participants from the general public (or "the community"). Most people generally, like most anarchists, and like most students of criminal justice, have heard little or nothing of RJ, as Sullivan & Tifft admit.[16] This

---

15 Kevin Passmore, *Fascism: A Very Short Introduction* (2nd ed.; Oxford: Oxford University Press, 2014), 65 (quoted); Richard Bessell, *Nazism and War* (New York: The Modern Library, 2006), 74–75.

16 Dennis Sullivan & Larry Tifft, "Introduction: The Healing Dimension of Restorative Justice: A One-World Body," *Handbook of Restorative Justice*, 6–7. Of course, they imagine (in 2006) that RJ is coming to be known, and coming into its own. Ibid., 7. As their bizarre subtitle indicates, Sullivan & Tifft have fully embraced the mysticism of the faith-based RJ advocates (with, to make matters worse, Marshall

is one reason why RJ programs persist undisturbed, off in a corner of the criminal justice system.[17] Nobody cares if they work or not. They work for those who work in them.

Restorative Justice, even as idealized by Tifft & Sullivan, is incompatible even with their own pacifism. Their statism, pacifism and mysticism are mutually incoherent, as well as incompatible with any type of anarchism. It is just as well that the anarchists are ignorant of RJ. But it is not so well that they have not advanced beyond their traditional, outdated and incomplete critique of law to envisage anarchist societies with disputing processes which are as voluntary as life in society allows for.

To my regret, the criminologists are finally trying to make some inroads among anarchists. On March 26–27, 2016, there was held the "1st Annual Anarchism, Crime, and Justice Conference at Fort Lewis College in Durango, Colorado, USA." According to the announcement:

> This conference is structured around challenging and abolishing punitive justice, while promoting community-based alternatives such as restorative justice, transformative justice and Hip Hop battling. . . .

Hip Hop battling?

There follows a long list of the standard leftist Social Justice Warrior issues: 27 "topics of interest." One of them is "green anarchism"; another is "anarchism."[18] Two workshops on anarchism out of 27. At this "anarchist" conference, as at some earlier ones, the anarchism is an afterthought. The organizer was Anthony Nocella II, whom I have previously abused here.

McLuhan thrown in). There were premonitions of this in *The Struggle to Be Human*, at 150, where they announced that "a spiritual awakening is necessary"—following this with a long quotation from Tolstoy.

17 "RJ remains on the periphery, exciting the intellects of academics and some practitioners, while the CJ system continues largely with business as usual, processing individuals through routine institutional practices and a set repertoire of responses." Cunneen, "Limitations of Restorative Justice," 122.

18 "Embarrassments to the Milieu," *Anarchy: A Journal of Desire Armed* No. 77 (2016), 68.

There is no suspicion that possibly "justice" itself has become, for modern anarchists, a problematic goal or value. The anarchist correct line on criminal justice, has now—unknown to the vast majority of anarchists—been authoritatively settled for them. Anarchists are to be for Restorative Justice, transformative justice and Hip Hop battling (whatever that is). I'm sure a few anarchists have heard of Hip Hop battling (I haven't, but I am an elderly white man), but probably not the other stuff. If it resembles the "song duels" among the Eskimos, who were anarchists—where disputants, face to face, sing insulting songs about each other, and the audience reacts—well, that might be *one* anarchist dispute resolution mechanism.[19] Another might be Hopi "grievance chants."[20] They all seem inappropriate, however, in cases of securities fraud, armed robbery, identity theft, homicide and rape.

Neighborhood Justice Centers were, I've argued, not a solution to any social problem. But I agree with their focus on disputes, not on crimes as such. Some crimes involve unilateral predation, not bilateral disputes. But most crimes, including most of the most feared crimes, arise from disputes. Restorative Justice and reintegrative shaming, although they purport to reject repressive, punitive justice, in fact fundamentally agree with its conservative, individualist, right-and-wrong, law-and-order, crime-and-punishment conception of interpersonal conflict. They are not even marketed as dispute resolution. Beware Mennonite probation officers and armed humanists (what Robespierre called "armed missionaries"). Shaming, officially administered, is obviously punishment. Just ask Hester Prynne. That conception, I've argued,[21] is incompatible with anarchism. And, anarchism aside, that approach is costly, cruel, oppressive, and even on its own terms a disastrous failure. The only within-the-system reform which

---

19 A. Adamson Hoebel, "Song Duels Among the Eskimo," *Law and Warfare*, 255–262.

20 Robert A. Black, "Hopi Grievance Chants: A Mechanism of Social Control," in *Studies in Southwestern Ethnolinguistics*, ed. Dell H. Hymes, William E. Bittle & Harry Hojer (The Hague & Paris: Mouton & Co., 1967), 7–11. No relation.

21 Black, "An Anarchist Response to 'The Anarchist Response to Crime.'"

would represent a substantial improvement would be substantial decriminalization, starting with the drug laws.[22] But less of more of the same is not enough. And, as of 2023, the Federal Government is still waging the War on Drugs.

In a modern anarchist society, as in primitive anarchist societies, the emphasis would be on dispute resolution, not on sin, guilt, shame, crime and punishment. There would be no law, especially no moralizing law such as Braithwaite and other conservatives endorse. Moralizing law is the major source of mass incarceration, police brutality and most violent crime. But it generates business for politicians, police, the private prison industry, Fox News commentators, organized crime, and for criminology professors—including the criminology professors who organize conferences on anarchism, criminology and justice.

Unless the anarchists offer a radical alternative, they will continue to be scorned. And rightly so.

---

[22] Edwin M. Schur, *Radical Non-Intervention* (Englewood Cliffs, NJ: Prentice-Hall, 1973). Braithwaite dislikes this book. He supports the drug laws. He writes: "The theory of reintegrative shaming implies that, rather than be tolerant and understanding, we should be intolerant and understanding." *Crime, Shame and Reintegration*, 166. He is intolerant but not understanding.

BOB BLACK is an American anarchist and essayist. He is the author of *The Abolition of Work and Other Essays*, *Beneath the Underground*, *Friendly Fire*, *Anarchy After Leftism*, *Defacing the Currency* and *The Myth of Human Rights*. His work has also appeared in countless zines and marginal publications.

Caveat Lector.

www.NineBandedBooks.com